DIARY OF A HARLEM SCHOOLTEACHER

OTHER BOOKS IN THE CLASSICS IN
PROGRESSIVE EDUCATION SERIES

Being with Children:
A High-Spirited Personal Account of
Teaching Writing, Theater, and Videotape
PHILLIP LOPATE

How Kindergarten Came to America:
Friedrich Froebel's Radical Vision of Early
Childhood Education
BERTHA VON MARENHOLTZ-BÜLOW

The New Education:
Progressive Education One Hundred Years Ago Today
SCOTT NEARING

The Public School and the Private Vision:
A Search for America in Education and Literature
MAXINE GREENE

Schoolmaster of the Great City:
A Progressive Educator's Pioneering Vision
for Urban Schools
ANGELO PATRI

DIARY OF A HARLEM SCHOOLTEACHER

JIM HASKINS

THE NEW PRESS

NEW YORK
LONDON

© 1979 by Jim Haskins
Series foreword © 2007 by Herbert Kohl
Foreword © 2008 by Herbert Kohl
All rights reserved.

Requests for permission to reproduce selections from this book should be
mailed to: Permissions Department, The New Press, 38 Greene Street,
New York, NY 10013.

Originally published in the United States by Grove Press, 1969
This edition published in the United States by The New Press, New York, 2008
Distributed by W. W. Norton & Company, Inc., New York

ISBN 978-1-59558-339-0
CIP data available

The New Press was established in 1990 as a not-for-profit alternative to the large,
commercial publishing houses currently dominating the book publishing industry.
The New Press operates in the public interest rather than for private gain, and is
committed to publishing, in innovative ways, works of educational, cultural, and
community value that are often deemed insufficiently profitable.

www.thenewpress.com

Composition by NK Graphics
This book was set in New Caledonia

Printed in Canada

2   4   6   8   10   9   7   5   3   1

To my mother

Education makes a people easy to lead, but difficult to drive; easy to govern, but impossible to enslave.

—Lord Brougham
House of Commons, 1828

Contents

Series foreword by Herbert Kohl   11

Foreword by Herbert Kohl   13

Acknowledgments   21

Introduction   23

1. FALL   31

2. WINTER   57

3. SPRING   93

4. NINE CHILDREN   139

Afterword   159

SERIES FOREWORD
Classics in
Progressive Education

My first classroom was empty. Not a book, piece of paper, pencil, or stick of chalk was in sight. The principal welcomed me to the school and informed me he had high expectations for each and every student. Crazy. I figured I had to dig into my meager savings and buy pencils, some remaindered typing paper, and discount crayons. Books were out of the question.

It was rough going for my first week of teaching, but during my second, two older female teachers showed up in my classroom after school. It turns out they were watching me and decided I might be a lifer—a lifelong progressive education teacher. They brought me boxes of books, material about the United Federation of Teachers, and most of all, some classics of progressive education. Over coffee after school one day, they informed me that both of them would retire in a year but wanted to keep the tradition of democratic, student-centered education alive. These teachers hoped to keep arts in the schools and they hoped that young teachers like me (I was 23 at the time) would keep the tradition going. But, they emphasized, in order to keep a tradition alive, you had to know its history and read its literature. That's why, in addition to all the specific educational material these teachers brought me, they insisted I read Dewey, Froebel, Freinet, Homer Lane, Makarenko, and many other democratic educators whose work has had major influences on educators throughout the world. Their teaching was concrete and their vision for education was large.

I didn't have a chance to thank these two teachers because

they retired in the middle of my first year of teaching without leaving their names or addresses. But I have honored their commitment to children and to progressive education. This series is meant to show them my appreciation for their unsolicited gifts to me.

This series will reissue important but often hard-to-find works of progressive education which are still very useful to people teaching today. It is essential to connect to tradition, to know that you are not alone trying to fight against authoritarian or corporate education. The goal is to energize teachers through a connection to educators who have struggled for democratic and creative education against the demands of governments, the rigidity of some churches, and the complex lives many students are forced to bear. The books reprinted are for teachers of hope who understand the complexities of struggling for their students and who might need a dose of history, a bit of humor, and lots of new ideas.

—Herbert Kohl
February 2007

Foreword

Diary of a Harlem Schoolteacher was written in 1969 by Jim Haskins, an African American teacher who was born in Demopolis, Alabama, in 1941. Over the years he taught elementary school and junior high school and taught remedial education courses. In 1977 he joined the English Department of the University of Florida, where he taught until his death in 2005.

Haskins also authored over one hundred books, many for young children and adolescents. The titles of some of his books illustrate his commitment to documenting the many facets of African American life and history in the United States. They show how wide his concerns were and how easily he moved from history or politics to biography, and from young children's counting books to ghost stories and adult literature. Here are just a few of the titles he authored: *The Headless Haunt and Other African American Ghost Stories* (HarperCollins, 1994), *Black Eagles: African Americans in Aviation* (Scholastic, 1995), *Get On Board: The Story of the Underground Railroad* (Scholastic, 1995), *Power to the People: The Rise and Fall of the Black Panther Party* (Simon & Schuster, 1997), *Spike Lee: By Any Means Necessary* (Walker, 1997), and *Black, Blue, and Gray: African Americans in the Civil War* (Simon & Schuster, 1998). He also wrote biographies of the Scottsboro Boys, John Lewis, Colin Powell, Stevie Wonder, and was co-author with Rosa Parks of her autobiography *Rosa Parks: My Story* (A Puffin Book, 2005). Just before his untimely death he was working on a biography of the baseball player Ernie Banks.

Jim Haskins wasn't a prominent author when he was a first-year teacher at PS 92 on 134th Street in Central Harlem in the fall of 1967. He described his decision to become a teacher and keep a diary of his experience, which became this book, in the following way:

> I started this diary as a personal document after coming into teaching from a Wall Street brokerage firm. I felt that I wanted to become a part of a larger human experience and in some small way make a contribution to that experience. I was soon to discover that under the then present and still going strong bureaucracy, doing that was almost impossible unless one was willing to become a part of that bureaucracy. I chose not to and in short order found myself, along with a few other young teachers, alienated, our hands tied, unable to offer suggestions or bring about change. After grappling with the decision to remain or get out I decided to record in this diary, hoping it would help calm my frustrations (21).

The student body was 98 percent black and 2 percent Puerto Rican. PS 92 was a new school building at the time—all the students and staff of PS 119, which was located in a rundown building not far away, were transferred to PS 92 the semester before Haskins began to teach.

Nat Hentoff, in *Does Anyone Give a Damn?*, described the desperate situation that had been festering at 119 for years and that led to the building of the new school:

> In 1961 . . . in a move unprecedented in the history of the New York public schools, PS 119's staff placed an ad in the now-defunct *World-Telegram* listing in appalling detail— from the prevalence of rats and roaches to sagging walls and unsanitary children's toilets—the dangerous deterioration of their bleak, fortresslike school building which had been erected in 1899.°

°Nat Hentoff, *Does Anyone Give a Damn?* (New York: Alfred Knopf, 1977), 205.

The new school was finally built after a large rat ran across the stage while Mayor Robert Wagner was visiting PS 119.

Hentoff described the move from the old school to PS 92, where James Haskins was to be a new teacher, in the following way:

> On the afternoon before the move, in the yard of PS 119, Elliot Shapiro (the Principal) announced that this would be everyone's last day at the old school, which was going to be torn down and turned into a playground for PS 92.
>
> An explosion of cheering was triggered by his announcement. "I was kind of surprised," Shapiro said later, "by such a unanimous expression of strong feeling. Sometimes, after all, you think nostalgically about an old school. But the cheering signified we were all worn out by this building. When we lined up the next morning," he continued, "the children were all in high spirits. There was an irresistible eagerness to get going and a lack of desire to look back. I felt the same way. To be sure, I had spent twelve years in that building, and you might have thought I'd have a touch of regret at leaving it. But like the children and the staff, I was glad to put it—even to push it—into the past."[*]

Hentoff ends *Our Children Are Dying* by noting, "PS 119 is being torn down. How many children since 1899 have already been buried there?"[†]

The old school, despite its physical structure, had a decent reputation among educators in New York City because of its charismatic principal. Shapiro was regarded by many progressive educators as being one of the most caring and creative principals in the system. According to Hentoff, Shapiro was a supportive, understanding leader of teachers and children. He was also supposed to have had warm relationships with parents and community groups and used some mothers as volunteer aides in the

[*]Nat Hentoff, *Our Children Are Dying* (Penguin Books, 1967), 135.
[†]Ibid., 140.

school. The school also had highly developed counseling services and established as a policy that no child would be suspended or expelled. All problems were to be adjudicated within the school by the staff and principal along with parents and students. In addition, teachers were encouraged to recognize that the learning styles of children differ and that therefore the curriculum had to be adjusted to the ways students learned.

Shapiro set up satellite storefront classrooms throughout the community in order to make the school a greater part of the neighborhood, and teachers made visits to parents after school hours. School tone and morale were central forces in Shapiro's work, and PS 119 had a reputation of being a "nice" school, a "good place to teach," despite its dismal physical conditions. It was supposed to be a model of the hope progressive educational practice can provide for poor children of color. Still, it is striking that the title of Hentoff's book is *The Children Are Dying*.

Despite the good morale at the school, the caring and supportive ways with children, and the outreach to the community, the students still did not learn to read, or do math and science. The academic performance of the students was abysmal. More attention was paid to ambiance and tone than to instruction. The teachers' lives were easier and more satisfying than they would be at more demoralized and chaotic schools; but this emphasis on developing a peaceful, supportive, and indulgent environment rather than a demanding academic one is at the base of current rejections of progressive ideas. Progressive education, often mistakenly, is confused with permissive education or libertarian education. This had led many educators to swing to the other side and emphasize rigid standards, high-stakes testing, teacher-proof curricula, and strict discipline. One wonders whether it is possible to be both supportive and nurturing at the same time as delivering effective instruction. Is it possible to build humane, creative educational institutions that develop academic skills as well as self-confidence, self-discipline, and a cooperative, democratic spirit? This is perhaps the most important issue facing progressive educators today.

Elliot Shapiro was no longer principal when Jim Haskins began teaching at PS 92. In 1967 Haskins entered the new school
with high expectations which were quickly shattered. According
to Haskins, "The school, as approached from the street, has the
appearance of a fort. It is a rectangular structure with a garden
and a very colorful mosaic courtyard inside its walls. (The children were not allowed to use the courtyard, however)" (26). It
was like an off-limits garden in the midst of a maximum-security
prison.

Without Shapiro's leadership there also seems to have been a
regression to the horrible norm of Harlem schools at the time—
disorder, serious discipline problems, academic failure, and de-
moralization despite the new building. The physical plant did
not solve the academic problems. What was left, according to
Haskins, was a permissiveness that bordered on the irresponsi-
ble. Students were indulged, pampered, even bribed to behave
decently. As an example, he tells the story of one of his students,
Wilbert, who in the past had been a coddled troublemaker. The
school secretary kept candy in her desk and whenever Wilbert
was sent to the principal's office she gave it to him to calm him
down. He must certainly have learned that these were the only re-
wards he would receive at the school—that is, until he entered Jim
Haskins' class. Haskins stopped the candy bribe and wouldn't halt
his teaching to attend to Wilbert's outrageous demands. Wilbert's
choice was to sit down and join in the class's activities or go to the
principal's office and sit doing nothing. No candy, no pampering.
What Haskins set up for Wilbert was a structure that moved
Wilbert back into the classroom rather than pushed him out of it.
Haskins didn't indulge him, nor did he reject him. Instead, he let
Wilbert know he had high standards for him and provided the
support Wilbert needed to make the transition from dysfunc-
tional defiant behavior to focused self-disciplined learning. He
had his student's long-term interests in mind and patiently welcomed Wilbert to be a member of the community of learners in
his class. Firmness and welcome seemed to be a formula that
worked for Haskins. According to him,

Eventually Wilbert came to understand that there were others in the class who also needed my help. He finally acclimated himself to class participation and is doing well now. He has gained self-control and his reading and math have improved. Now, Wilbert has been retested and, I hope, will be assigned to a regular class.

He is well motivated and seemingly delights in his newfound confidence in himself. This attitude has offset many of the problems he has at home. Recently, when a fire in his building kept all of the children out of school, Wilbert cried, his mother reported, until she had to agree to send him to school at noon.

Wilbert probably benefited from the small-class situation but not from the CRMD (Children with Retarded Mental Development) class itself. He could have been severely retarded if steps had not been taken to stop his tantrums and get him engaged in meaningful work (158).

Elsewhere in the *Diary*, Haskins remarks that

Many teachers admit that the school is really controlled by the students. They call it "the snake pit" or "the ship of fools" because so many teachers appear on the edge of a mental breakdown. About four teachers who have been "released from duties" at other schools have found a home here (102).

In other words, teachers whom no other school wanted were dumped at PS 92 because it was new and had a new principal. They had tenure, were thrown out of other schools, and were protected by union tenure rules. They had to be placed somewhere regardless of the effects they might have on their students. Haskins and a few other new teachers were fighting against this practice and other practices. They tried to teach well within a defective school system at a school dominated by a demoralized staff.

Diary of a Harlem Schoolteacher is a very bitter book written by a very loving man. What Haskins experienced at PS 92 in Harlem in the 1960s reminds me of the schools Jonathan Kozol described in *Savage Inequalities* more than twenty years later. The relationships between black and white teachers at PS 92 are also reminiscent of the relationship between black and white teachers described in Lisa Delpit's *Other People's Children.* What is unique about Haskins's book, though, is that it is a report from the front, an ongoing account of what happened in one school, at a particular historical moment, from the perspective of one teacher who believed in the potential of the children and was appalled both by student behavior at the school and by the way teachers responded to it. More essentially, it is the only published diary I know of written by a black teacher who was sensitive to the needs, capacities, and culture of the students and aware of the complex racial tension and bureaucratic neglect that characterize a failing school purporting to serve poor, predominantly black students. Haskins was in a unique position to comprehend the complexities faced by white teachers who didn't understand their students or their culture, and who had low expectations for them.

In the second edition of the book, published in 1979, ten years after the original edition was published, Haskins says in a new introduction, "This diary reports the events that happened during a typical Harlem school year as observed by me, a black teacher, a decade ago. It is a diary that, unfortunately, could have been written last year" (27). And I have to admit, from what I have observed over that past few years, it could equally have been written now, in 2008, almost forty years later.

The author's passion and concern for the children and his continued commitment to them no matter how poorly they might have been educated is remarkable. His candid way of expressing his doubts and frustrations provide a portrait of what it is really like to teach in a failing inner-city school.

The book raises questions about skills teaching, direct instruction, the role of culture in learning, and the role of discipline in the promotion of learning that progressive educators must respond to. It is necessary for progressives to listen to multiple voices and reconceptualize progressive practice in a way that embraces the complex racial, ethnic, and class problems that are manifested in the schools. The book is worth reading and thinking about today as a dramatic reminder of how little educational progress has been made over the past forty years, and how much educational work there is still to do.

—Herbert Kohl
January 2008

Acknowledgments

I started this diary as a personal document after coming into teaching from a Wall Street brokerage firm. I felt that I wanted to become a part of a larger human experience and in some small way make a contribution to that experience. I was soon to discover that under the then present and still going strong bureaucracy, doing that was almost impossible unless one was willing to become a part of that bureaucracy. I chose not to and in short order found myself, along with a few other young teachers, alienated, our hands tied, unable to offer suggestions or bring about change. After grappling with the decision to remain or get out I decided to record this diary, hoping it would help calm my frustrations.

The published version does not differ substantially from the original. When I showed some of the early entries to Fran Morrill, a school social worker, she presented me with a large diary book in which I could keep a more organized and accurate record of what I thought then might be my final year in the New York City school system, and suggested that I publish it.

I am also indebted to Lynn Haines, who painstakingly translated my handwriting so that Bonny Persons could type the early manuscript. Dolores Brooks gave generously of her time and experience as a school psychologist in constructive criticism. Many others were helpful, and I especially want to thank Helen Churney, Eileen Allgeyer, Nat Hentoff, and Al Levy. A special thanks to Julius Lester, whose suggestions on the final draft were of great help.

Nothing in this diary should be interpreted as necessarily representing the opinions or judgments of anyone other than the diarist.

All the names used in the diary are fictitious, except the name of the diarist.

—J.H.

Introduction

In the late 1960s Rhody McCoy was the beleaguered administrator of Brooklyn's Ocean Hill–Brownsville School District, an experiment in school decentralization designed to give individual communities more control over their own schools, including the hiring and firing of teachers and principals and authority over budgetary matters and organizational concerns. The idea behind the experiment was that black and Hispanic children could not learn in a system foisted on them by the white bureaucracy and that their parents and members of their communities, being more aware of and concerned about their needs, could, if given the opportunity, create a better system. It was a perfectly reasonable idea, and though McCoy was constantly harassed and beset by the difficulties of reconciling conflicting interest groups in his district, he was hopeful, in 1969, that it was an idea that could be made to work.

But that was in the late 1960s when, fresh from a spate of civil rights victories and happily contemplating the future benefits of affirmative action programs, we blacks were confident that we could indeed wrest control of the institutions that held sway over us, and that we would do a better job operating these institutions than our white predecessors had. The assassinations of Malcolm X, Martin Luther King Jr., and Robert Kennedy had clouded our vision of Camelot somewhat, but we hadn't expected the road to be easy.

What we did expect was progress. Products of the twentieth century that we were, we just naturally assumed that progress was inevitable. "You can't turn back the hands of the clock," we'd say. So we were hopeful and, in retrospect, hopelessly naive.

"Black people know that they have been had educationally," I concluded, "and that the system can never return to business as usual."

"In this point of transition the black community is determined to destroy its traditional paternalistic dependency on the white community," wrote McCoy.

Ten years later, neither of us is in the New York City public school system. Rhody McCoy went on to teach at the University of Massachusetts. I went on to college teaching, too. Ten years later, it's still business as usual in that system, and black and Hispanic children are just as ill-educated and exploited as ever. The system has proved stronger than those who would change it; its continuation seems as inevitable as death and taxes. What it has not managed to keep out or destroy, it has co-opted.

It is ironic that just when black people started to seize control of the schools in their communities, New York City was plunged into the worst financial crisis in its history. There was hardly enough to maintain traditional programs; the brave new experiments went quickly by the wayside. The MES (More Effective Schools) program, for example, called for smaller class sizes and two teachers for each class of culturally deprived (read: minority) children. But with the city on the verge of bankruptcy, teachers were laid off by the thousands, and because seniority was the determining factor in who got laid off and who didn't, it was the younger teachers—some of the best and the brightest—and a large proportion of the newly hired minority teachers who were let go, leaving the jaded, unenthusiastic, just-ten-more-years-and-I'll-be-eligible-to-collect-my-pension teachers to preside over classrooms whose registers reached forty children or more. That didn't leave the communities much room to exercise their newly won power to hire and fire.

Control over a budget has little meaning when that budget is a shrinking one. The scramble after pie crumbs can get downright vicious. We learned that lesson well. Turns out that minority people can be corrupted by power quite as quickly and thoroughly as whites, especially at a time when there is much less power to go around and so many groups after what little there is. Back in 1969, the decentralization controversy was primarily a matter of black versus white; since then, Hispanics, women, the handicapped, and in some areas Native Americans, have claimed their rights as minorities, too. The resulting scandals have angered community parents equally as much as the evidence of the abuse of power on the part of white administrators did—more so, in fact, because the minority leaders were supposed to be inherently more moral and less corruptible. So were the minority teachers who managed to escape the fiscal purge. But they were holding on to their jobs for dear life, and no other circumstance guarantees better the loss of originality and enthusiasm. Concerned as they were about mere survival, they became just as committed to their own vested interests and to maintaining the status quo as the whites—and just as uncommitted to educating their young charges.

Visit a Harlem school at 9:15 A.M. any school day, without prior notice, and you'll find teachers sitting at their desks reading the newspaper while their pupils stand pledging their allegiance to the flag. Go to a museum on a schoolday morning and watch teachers allow their children to run undisciplined through the galleries and halls while they find a bench to sit on or go somewhere to have a cigarette. Is it any wonder that the children are not being educated? Is it any wonder that they do not respect their teachers? The only wonder is that we could be so sure, ten years ago, that things would get better. But back then, it seemed that the only way to go was up. At least that's the way it seemed to one teacher at PS 92 Manhattan.

Public School 92 is on 134th Street, in the heart of Central Harlem. Ten years ago, the area was almost totally blighted with the exception of a new school plant, which, incidentally, was built after a large rat ran across the stage while Mayor Robert Wagner was visiting the old school a few years earlier. Though new, the school already had a number of broken windows.

The school, as approached from the street, has the appearance of a fort. It is a rectangular structure with a garden and a very colorful mosaic courtyard inside its walls. (The children were not allowed to use the courtyard, however.) A teacher whose classroom was on the back side of the building could look down into this beautiful court and for a few moments forget completely the fact that his or her classroom was in the middle of Harlem. Next door, the new St. Philip's Episcopal Church community center was nearing completion. A few funeral homes dotted the block along with several deserted buildings, long ago abandoned by their landlords and tenants. A few local entrepreneurs had candy stores in their homes which they opened only at lunchtime to catch the school trade. The children would flock to these make-shift stores to purchase such expensive goodies as one-cent gum (three in a pack) and pencils that were monogrammed for an insurance company that did and still does a great deal of burial service in Harlem. (Most Harlem residents prefer the low-cost burial policies instead of life insurance because they are generally cheaper.) Most of these candy stores were unlicensed and poorly stocked.

At the time, 98 percent of PS 92's thousand students were black and came from families whose total income was far below the federal poverty income level. Their fathers sat on the stoops and stared at the broken classroom windows, behind which sat their children. Occasionally, the men would walk down to the construction site where the new playground was nearing completion. They would help lift large boulders too heavy for the laborers to lift alone, and then drift back aimlessly to their stoops. They were as starved for work as their children were starved for education. A few women went out to jobs downtown, but most of them sat looking out their windows at the school or the streets below.

The other two percent of the population of PS 92 were Puerto Rican, who for the most part lived in the city housing projects. Those from the housing projects constituted our middle-class children in the area, even though a large percentage of project dwellers also existed on income below federal standards. We had long since lost our one percent Chinese population to Montessori-type schools.

The area was infested with drug addicts—many still in their teens and many who were familiar to older teachers as a result of having been in their classes. There was an uneven proportion of emotionally disturbed children in the school due to the fact that P.S. 92 received an uneven number of disturbed children suspended from other schools in its district. That stemmed from the Shapiro days, when the school was thought to be the center for children with problems. No child was turned away. Elliott Shapiro, who was principal for several years, felt he had many of the answers to the problems of ghetto children, and the administration was still reluctant to suspend any pupil for any reason—perhaps out of fear of tarnishing its already dubious record of never having suspended a child.

This diary reports the events that happened during a typical Harlem school year as observed by me, a black teacher, a decade ago. It is a diary that, unfortunately, could have been written last year.

DIARY OF A HARLEM
SCHOOLTEACHER

1
Fall

FRIDAY

September 29

Today was the start of the new school year, after the thirteen-day United Federation of Teachers's strike. The same CRMD° class I taught last term was assigned to me again. Nine familiar faces were present, plus two new ones. The school attendance for the beginning of a new year was poor.

Everything else is as usual—missing items because of my classroom being used over the summer, a few broken windows, and an assortment of distasteful graffiti on the blackboards, written with wax crayon.

The parents of the two new students came in, both smelling of whisky and in a hurry to get out and leave their children in my hands. Neither of the two children had had breakfast, or a summer that was worth remembering.

The teachers were in a hurry to get away and enjoy a few more hours of freedom before starting the long and difficult year ahead. There are a few new faces among the teachers, replacing those who have transferred, quit, or retired.

• • •

MONDAY

October 2

Received three more new students today, all without records. The Board of Education or their old school doesn't seem to realize the necessity for the new teacher of transfer students to have their records on hand.

Our classroom was broken into over the weekend, as were the

°Children with Retarded Mental Development. CRMD classes are set up according to age and I.Q., not grade level. The children in my class ranged in age from nine to eleven.

rooms on the second floor. Nothing was taken. However, the glass in the door and several locks on closets were broken.

Using rags and gasoline, I finally cleaned the blackboards of all the crayoned dirty words.

Still no supplies or issuance of books. And still no introduction of the new staff to the teaching body. Maybe tomorrow.

The assistant principal has started off the year as usual. He has his little black notebook in which he jots down things to be remembered. He came into my room to ask about books and materials. He wrote in his book that I had none and asked me to place a note to that effect in his box.

• • •

TUESDAY

October 3

Class size is now up to fourteen, plus one student who was in my class last year. He was causing a behavior problem in his new teacher's room.

Supplies arrived today. They were ordered by the teacher who had this class last year. Most of the materials are art-oriented. Although I am not artistically inclined, I have to keep them. I should make use of the materials or they will simply remain in the cabinets.

I'll have to wait until next year for the supplies I ordered this year. The CRMD teachers have a special supply fund or budget and, except for such things as paper and chalk, we cannot get our materials from the general supply.

The school secretary discovered today that the school bell does not work.

• • •

WEDNESDAY
October 4

Today was the last day before the two-day Jewish holiday. The students sensed the mood of the staff—they knew it would be an easy day, with no homework assignments over the holiday.

Four school days have passed and still no class schedules or a visit from the area supervisor or our resource teacher° to coordinate the CRMD classes. The latter is ill in Tennessee and a substitute has not yet been assigned.

The result is that school has started with a loss of four preparation periods. We probably will not get them made up even when the resource teacher arrives.

• • •

MONDAY
October 9

Class size reached the fifteen CRMD maximum today. There is a complete lack of coordination from the district CRMD supervisor. The morale of most of the faculty is very low, mostly because of the strike this fall. There are divided opinions on the strike, and two camps have emerged. Those in the camp which supported the strike either agree with the union's position or are simply pro-union. Those in the other camp did not support the strike and have become anti-union.

I have begun to think seriously about leaving the system at the end of the school year.

I met a former teacher today whose entire time while teaching last year was spent writing a book on his class. He is doing addi-

---

°Usually a senior teacher appointed by the supervisor to work with all the CRMD teachers in a school. Also known as a cluster or OTP (Other Teachers' Programs) teacher, the resource teacher relieves other teachers during the periods allowed daily for lesson preparation and rest.

tional research for his book now, before going into the Peace Corps to escape the draft.

There are many young men in this and other ghetto schools who are teaching in order to avoid the draft. Many will leave after they pass draft age, to go on to graduate school. Some will stay and become committed to teaching. The few who stay will do so because it is hard to leave the children who need help so desperately.

• • •

TUESDAY

October 10

Arthur, who has been to school only thirty-six days in four years, was present today. He has been in my class since the latter half of last year, when he was present only ten days.

Arthur has a sister in the CRMD class for older pupils. In contrast to his attendance record, she came to school almost every day last year.

Arthur gets lost on his way to school or stays home and sleeps. His parents do not attempt to make him come to school. His attendance record has been the same all of his school career.

His retardation is more social than psychological. The guidance people have been unable or unwilling to do anything about his problem, and he continues to slip endlessly into a sea of ignorance.

• • •

WEDNESDAY

October 11

I met with a white psychologist from Harlem Hospital today. He is from Australia and is trying to set up a program for children with emotional problems. After listening to him for an hour over lunch, I realized that he has a limited knowledge of children from deprived neighborhoods.

There was a fight today between a teacher and a child's parent, who invited the teacher outside. The story is that yesterday the teacher struck the child on his hand and made it bleed.

The incident was a matter for the principal's office, but no action was taken in defense of the teacher and the problem was not resolved. Actually, the boy had a sore on his hand and bumped it while sidestepping the teacher. The parent should have gone to the office before confronting the teacher, so that the principal could have avoided this fight.

School will be closed tomorrow, Columbus Day.

• • •

FRIDAY

October 13

Not much happened today, probably because many children stayed home, making it one of those long weekends.

Friday is our scheduled assembly day, and, as usual, we had to deal with behavior problems. Many teachers, mostly white, believe that the children should be allowed to run and play in assembly. Others, mostly black, disagree. Thus there is constant conflict over the proper method of conducting assembly. Generally the white teachers tend to be excessively permissive with their students while black teachers are more concerned with structured assemblies.

Arthur is out again today.

I've sent cards to the parents of the absent children, Arthur and the two new kids, in case they are playing hooky.

The school decentralization project is becoming an issue in our school, and it is beginning to cause a different kind of split among the faculty. White teachers appear not to trust black teachers' sense of fair play as far as the decentralization issue is concerned.

• • •

MONDAY

October 16

Monday is always a hard day for everyone who works; it seems additionally difficult for those of us who teach. The children have had a two-day rest and are full of energy; it takes time to settle them down.

They have a lot to say about their weekend—fires, stabbings, the police, etc. Usually the assignment is to let them tell the class "what happened on my block over the weekend." After the discussion I have them write a short composition on their experiences. They thus have the opportunity to learn the correct spelling of the words they use.

Wilbert saw a man cut to death on the corner of Eighth Avenue and 130th Street. He was very upset; telling about the incident, he talked rapidly and stuttered.

Arthur is still out. I reported the problem to the guidance counselor, who will handle it from here on, I hope.

• • •

TUESDAY

October 17

We had visitors from Pennsylvania today. They were all white and many of them participate in the "Fresh Air" program instituted by the now defunct *Herald Tribune*. Many of our students have spent part of their summers with some of these families.

They came to see the school and neighborhood of their summer visitors. Many were shocked at the blighted area. Others were not.

"It was just as they told me," one matron said. "Very bad and very sad," one man said. "I feel so very sorry." "Why does the city allow these people to live in those buildings?" one woman asked.

Some of the visitors brought their own children with them. There were happy greetings and conversation among the children, recalling the summer weeks they had shared. Many brought gifts of clothes and books.

· · ·

WEDNESDAY

October 18

Because of the rainy weather four out of the fifteen in my class stayed home.

Melvin's mother thought he was in school yesterday and today. She came for him before three o'clock, and called up to my window to ask if I would excuse him early. I told her he was not in school today. She then made an excuse for him—"I forgot, I let him go to a cadet meeting."

Yesterday I had my pupils take home form letters asking the parents to see me about their children's work. None of them has responded; maybe tomorrow. Some will not come, others will make very elaborate excuses, and a few will show up. You get to know who will respond and who will not. You also hope that you won't start condemning the child whose parent doesn't respond.

· · ·

THURSDAY

October 19

Two mothers came in today. One of them has a son who is no longer in my class; he was transferred to a younger level. She said she could not talk to the new teacher, who is white, the way she talks to me. She had been drinking, and she probably meant that if she were to talk to the white teacher she would be embarrassed, whereas I "would understand."

The other parent proposed that whipping her daughter would

improve her ability to learn. When I told her this would not help, and that Rachel needed more supervision at home and help every night, she replied that she had others at home and did not have the time. I suggested that perhaps the older children could help Rachel. The mother agreed, looked relieved, and left.

Arthur's sister brought in a note from their mother today. Arthur is sick but he will be back to school on Monday.

• • •

FRIDAY

October 20

TGIF (Thank God It's Friday) is the most popular phrase among the teachers. It's usually the salutation to start off all Fridays.

For the most part Fridays are uneventful—unless, of course, they fall on the first or the fifteenth, which are welfare check days and city paydays. Then the whole neighborhood takes on a kind of carnival atmosphere. As we leave the building at three we are met by men standing outside near the doors, offering to buy drinks for their children's teachers. People drink openly on the stoops and in the hallways, in full view of the children, who have to push their way past them to get home. The older girls are approached by wine-drinking fellows, some of them eighteen to twenty, who have dropped out of school.

• • •

MONDAY

October 23

All the students were present and full of stories about their weekend—spent, in the main, in the streets. We wrote our short compositions about the weekend experiences.

Only one child out of fifteen knows how to spell his father's name. The mother's name presents no difficulties. This holds true even though most pupils live with both parents.

Joe, who knows his father's name but can't spell it, uses his mother's maiden name instead of going by his father's surname.

Most of our students spend their time with their mothers and learn from them most of what they know before entering school. Generally the father works while the child is asleep. The general impression is that most fathers are absent from their homes entirely, but they aren't.

One boy's composition today read: "Over the week my little boy to [little brother's toe] wos bit by a rat. My mother too him to the hospital."

• • •

TUESDAY
October 24

Cherry was late today, as usual. She always has a little story about why she is late—she has to go to the washer or for the paper, or she does her homework in the morning.

A father who last week made an appointment through the principal to see me yesterday at ten has not yet shown up.

Taped school opening exercises are being piped into the classrooms. The children (probably the older classes as well) have not yet learned the national anthem or "America." The intent of these taped exercises is to teach the songs, when, in fact, the children don't listen anyway.

For many years, under the last principal, the emphasis was not on learning the standard materials most students must learn. The emphasis has shifted under the new principal and the children are learning new things, which, of course, for children in other areas are not new but expected. When a pupil walks up to the teacher and says, "Teacher, I know the national anthem!" he says it with a sense of pride and at the same time with an air of expecting reward. I usually show pleasure and congratulate him. Some teachers give money or candy.

• • •

WEDNESDAY
October 25

We are still having trouble getting the children to come to school on time. Most of them live in the neighborhood and the only ones who take buses are a few of the CRMD pupils.

Alvin, a fat little fellow, sleeps every morning until eight and does not have time to wash his face until he gets to school. I brought combs, oil, lotion, and face towels from home for the children to use for such emergencies.

We have an addition to our classroom, a caged hamster. The children decided to name him Mr. Haskins. The hamster was donated by a Hunter College student who has been helping the children learn to read. She is devoted to our class and to the two other retarded classes.

• • •

THURSDAY
October 26

We received a new student, Jackie, in our class, which now has an actual total of sixteen. For retarded children that's a lot. Jackie, however, although very slow, is not, in my judgment, retarded. She has not been tested CRMD, but the guidance counselor felt my class would be more suitable because the regular third-grade teacher does not want her in her class. (She does not respond or relate to the teacher.)

This situation is against regulations but is not irregular in our school. Under ordinary circumstances Jackie would be deemed a "disruptive child" because she does not function well in large classes. So far we have had no trouble. Although she is handicapped in the physiological sense, until she is tested and assigned to a CRMD class she is not officially enrolled.

Jackie is "tongue-tied" and suffers from an emotional instability that requires immediate attention. This, of course, will not be handled immediately because there is a six-months-to-a-year psychologist's waiting list.

• • •

FRIDAY
October 27

I was told today that I would be receiving two more students on Monday, even though, officially, I now have fifteen, the maximum for CRMD classes. Like Jackie, the two are to sit in, but I may not carry them on my roll. I can't go to the union to complain because I did not support the strike; therefore I am out of good grace with the representative. And, of course, it would do no good to go to the Board of Ed.

I tried in vain to discuss with the guidance counselor some problems about the two new admissions, who are from a class down the hall. She could not be found at first and she did not have time for me when I found her later in the day.

Today I was assembly leader for the third grade. I couldn't get any cooperation from the other two male teachers on my grade level, who are white. I had to rush around and beg two flags from other teachers for the color guard. The two third-grade teachers were also unwilling to allow boys from their classes to carry the flags. I ended up getting two boys from another class. These two teachers are very permissive in dealing with their students. Their classes must have 90 percent more cavities than the rest of the students because they solve all their behavior problems with candy.

• • •

MONDAY

October 30

First thing this morning I went down to the guidance counselor to discuss the two children the principal assigned to my class on Friday.

Also, I wanted to discuss an after-school clinic at North Side, which one student in my class but not on my register attends. He is on sedatives, which affect his performance in class. The guidance counselor told me to discuss it with his mother. Although that is actually the counselor's job, I wrote to the mother asking her to come in to see me. She can't read, but perhaps a neighbor will read the note for her. I can't call her because there is no telephone in the house. The boy is brighter than most of my pupils, and if he can ever get off the sedatives that keep him glassy-eyed all day he can really make progress. He is not retarded, but he is disruptive when he is not drugged.

• • •

TUESDAY

October 31

Today is Halloween and we are having a party, as is customary in all schools. I introduced the children to bobbing for apples. They had never played the game before.

There were no tubs around and it was a real project getting the dietician to let us use one of her large pots.

Each child was asked to bring fifteen cents to contribute to the expense of the party. Most did not, and some brought only a nickel. We searched the neighborhood for a pumpkin and found one for seventy cents, which took all our money. I came to the rescue for the apples, candy, chips, and a few other goodies.

• • •

WEDNESDAY

November 1

There was a great deal of friction today between the two guidance counselors and the resource teacher for the CRMD classes, the guidance people insisting that disruptive students sit in CRMD classes.

I was informed by the principal today that my room is needed by the first grade. It has something to do with one first-grade teacher refusing to allow an extra teacher in her room, although that is Board of Ed policy now for ghetto first-graders. Probably she does not want another teacher to discover just how bad or good a teacher she is; or she doesn't want to participate in the Board's program for training new teachers. The principal has not acted on the problem, as though it will go away if it is not discussed.

I am reluctant to move my class to the third floor, where there are larger children. Nor has the room I'm expected to move into been prepared for occupancy. I suppose they think I'm going to clean it.

• • •

THURSDAY

November 2

Wilbert came to school crying this morning because his father had slapped him. He said his father wouldn't let him eat his breakfast because he was already late for school. When Wilbert refused to leave without breakfast, his father hit him.

Continued harassment to move to the third floor. The room there was the art classroom last year and still has excess chairs and desks and extra equipment scattered all over the place. The cabinets are filled with paints, brushes, and other art materials. There are also two large kilns in the back of the room.

The custodian has not removed anything. He says there is no storage room for any of this material and that he is not a member of the movers' union. I'm expected to move the accumulation of three years' CRMD supplies to a room now spilling over with art supplies.

• • •

FRIDAY
November 3

Before the day was over there were several irate parents in the school, cursing and shouting about their children's behavior problems. There was also a fight between two girls over a pack of gum.

I left school early, at one o'clock, almost at my wits' end trying to combat administrative maneuvering. All the principal and assistant principal had to do to avoid the mess was to stay in the general office, where the parents came to see them. Instead, when a cursing parent entered the door they disappeared. Certainly a lot of unpleasantness could have been avoided if the administrators had remained to defend the teachers, who had to stay on and take the abuse and obscenities that were heaped on them.

• • •

MONDAY
November 6

The principal finally won her campaign to get me to move. I suppose she succeeded because of my refusal to be brought into a direct confrontation over the issues.

I asked the custodian to move the materials out of the new room. He replied, "Tell the principal to ask me."

So we moved into the new room, pushing all excess materials to the side. Now we have our classes amid a great deal of junk.

School is closed tomorrow, Election Day.

• • •

WEDNESDAY
November 8

The extra chairs and tables and art supplies have not been removed.

The grandmother of one of the students came to school today to beat up a white teacher. We never found out what the conflict was all about. It probably was not much of anything.

All a white teacher has to do these days is stand up to a pupil and he's in a lot of trouble. Whatever their complaint, the parents who come to protest apparently have to shore up their courage with a drink first.

Two parents came in to see me today, the same ones who usually show up. Both continue to smell of whisky.

Arthur still has a sporadic attendance record.

I received a note from a parent who had kept her child out two days. She explained that there was no heat in the house, so they all stayed in bed until noon, because it was too cold to get up.

• • •

THURSDAY
November 9

During lunch today, while the children were playing in the street, Wilbert fell in some dog waste on the curb and started vomiting and crying. (We do not have a playground. One was promised last year, and then the officials said it would be open the start of this term.)

I had to fill out an accident form, even though obviously no accident occurred. There is a memo from the principal stating, "All accidents or 'happenings' must be reported, no matter how minor." It took twenty minutes of class time to do the report and ask the required questions, which made even the children laugh.

Ten teachers were absent today!

Because there aren't a sufficient number of substitutes who will teach in Harlem schools, all the classes suffer when teachers are absent. Those without teachers are split up among the other teachers, whose classes in many cases already exceed the maximum of thirty-five.

One of the substitutes who did come to work was caught by the principal allowing the children to pitch quarters. The sub was angry at her reprimand and probably will not come back when called again.

I had coffee this morning with a teacher whose son has left home to become a hippie and "find himself." I promised I would speak with him if I see him in the Village. (I know him from his frequent appearances at school.) He is a bright boy and I look forward to a good talk with him. One thing is for sure, this teacher's problems with her own children are not affecting her class. She is a good, dedicated teacher.

Nothing has been done yet about my classroom. If the mess is not moved out within a few more days I will be compelled to throw it all out into the hallway and refuse to allow anyone to put it back.

• • •

FRIDAY

November 10

The film *The Red Balloon* was shown at our regular assembly today. The children really enjoyed it.

Today is the last day of Open School Week, but none of the parents I really wanted to see came, even though I sent them notes along with the usual letters from the general office.

Most of the parents will not show up and a few will write to say they had other children to attend to, or had to go to another school to see the teacher of another child—which is true in most cases. Many parents have four or five children in different schools.

• • •

MONDAY
November 13

All the children were present today except Alvin, who has been ill with a cold for a week. They had their usual stories to tell about the weekend fights, fires, etc.

I spoke again today with the principal about the removal of the stuff in our new room. I told her I was going to put the mess in the hall if nothing was done. No response. I conferred with the custodian about the removal and he informed me again that his men were not members of the movers' union.

• • •

TUESDAY
November 14

Wilbert came to school in a bad emotional state. When I asked him why he was upset he said, "My father whips me too much," and began to cry.

This usually happens whenever his father feels well enough. Wilbert is in a constant state of fright. The father has a heart ailment and is sick most of the time. When he is well, he tries to pay the children back for the times he has missed. The children—there are three of them—all have serious emotional problems which will take time to correct, and there is that long waiting list at the clinics.

The surplus desks and chairs and all the other junk are still in the room. The mess doesn't help Wilbert's condition. Our cluttered classroom probably makes him feel more trapped and closed in than at home.

• • •

WEDNESDAY
November 15

The excess desks were finally removed, but not before the custodian, or engineer, as he prefers to be called, let me know what a great favor he was doing the class and me. The other articles remain in the room.

Wilbert started crying again when the children joked about his father. At the mere mention of his father's name he begins to cry. He said no when I asked him if he wanted me to talk to his father. He is probably afraid his father would whip him for telling me what happens at home.

Arthur is out again today. His sister says he left home to come to school. I visited their apartment but no one was home, or they didn't answer the door.

• • •

THURSDAY
November 16

A real split among the black and white teachers has started over the appointment of a Negro as principal. She has been acting principal for two years in the absence of the last principal. This school has never had a black principal.

There have been several meetings of black teachers which the white teachers were not asked to attend, although some did. Many whites felt hurt and rejected, and started rumors that the black teachers are antiwhite racists. At clock-out time there was considerable distance between the white and black teachers. One white teacher I know very well did not speak to me, even though she knows how I feel.

Today I refused to attend a "closed" meeting. I felt that since we teachers are asked to function as a unit, all the teachers should have been asked to the meeting. Instead it turned into a black unit for a black principal.

• • •

FRIDAY

November 17

The teacher split is continuing. However, many whites who do not usually speak are attempting polite smiles. The break is probably good if it makes the numerous teachers who usually just sit and read (both white and black) get interested in discussing problems—and ultimately get down to the business of the children's welfare.

One of the many subordinate reasons for the break is that a good number of white teachers in the higher grades encourage students to visit them when they leave or graduate. Ninety percent of our students go to the junior high school three blocks away; they come back on their lunch hour and stay to help their former teachers, going to the store for them for sodas or lunch—which, of course, is against Board directives. This was just one of the many complaints that came out of the closed meeting yesterday.

A lot of things are coming out into the open, some good but mostly bad.

• • •

MONDAY

November 20

The black teachers have been holding meetings with the parents. Today the parents came to school to meet with them. The parents don't care if the white teachers are upset about not being included in the meeting. Many stated emphatically, "The whites have a nerve, with their all-Jewish meetings that blacks are not invited to!" The reference is to the Jewish Teachers' Association.

The parents marched on the district office (which is only six blocks away), but they received no satisfaction from the district superintendent, who seems to be all for appointing a Jewish principal.

Note: All the principals in this district are Jewish.

The whole problem of school decentralization is in open, hot debate. Most white teachers feel that there is no need for decentralization and that the present system is adequate. The black teachers believe the status quo is inadequate because it is crippling black children. Decentralization or not, the real problems are much deeper.

• • •

TUESDAY
November 21

The parents are preparing for a long fight to get the acting principal appointed principal. She has passed the examination for the position and is twentieth on the city civil-service list. The parents say they will not accept any other person for the job. The district superintendent has advised the superintendent of schools that he has solved the problem and has pleased the parents, who are anything but pleased at this moment and are preparing to ask for the district superintendent's resignation.

There is increasing bitterness between white and black teachers. If it continues it will further affect the children. Many teachers were already unhappy working here and are using this confrontation as an excuse for further resentment.

• • •

WEDNESDAY

November 22

Thank God for the two-day holiday, which starts tomorrow!

The parents are claiming that if they are not listened to in the selection of the principal, they will make IS 201 look like a picnic (referring to the school in East Harlem which has had its share of troubles).

Many of the teachers feel that the parents' attempt to get their choice appointed will fall on deaf ears. I am inclined to go along with them, knowing the entrenched methodology of the Board.

We had a false fire drill today. We were in the street before the announcement came that it was a false alarm.

• • •

MONDAY

November 27

Apparently the parents' meetings in school have been stopped, for now the meetings are being held in the church next door. Still only blacks are being asked to attend. The parents are distrustful of the whites, who, they feel, will sabotage their plans to get a black principal.

Although many parents really like many of the white teachers, they nevertheless believe that white feelings toward them are benevolent and paternalistic at best. They must show the whites that they can act politically without their help.

Many blacks—both parents and teachers—believe that with the advent of school decentralization most of their problems will be solved. If they have a say in the selection of principals to head their schools, they certainly could not do any worse than the Board has done. In this case the parents have an excellent candidate (even though I have disagreed with her decisions many times).

• • •

TUESDAY
November 28

The parents are considering a student boycott to press their demands for the acting principal's appointment. They have met again with the district superintendent, who is not responsive to their demands. A district school board meeting is to be held tonight. No doubt it will result in further confusion.

The split among the teachers is continuing. An article in the *Amsterdam News* about the principalship appointment included parent criticism of some teachers' manner of dress, mainly the miniskirt, and in one case of a teacher's body odor. The newspaper quotations were hostile to the white teachers.

• • •

WEDNESDAY
November 29

Confusion and bitterness were the order of business last night at the school board meeting. There were many white teachers from our school, although only one white, a woman, got up to protest the "horrible" lies that were being told to the community by the district superintendent. The whites' failure to speak up was not exactly greeted with open arms by the parents or the black teachers.

Conversation between blacks and whites on any subject is now hard to come by. A few months ago at least it was fashionable to enter into a dialogue on Mississippi or civil rights, and even to plan parties in the teachers' lunchroom. Not anymore.

On the TV news tonight it became apparent, to me at least, that the battle over who is going to get the job of principal has only begun. The Board seems to have reneged on the promise the parents thought they had won.

The Board will react in its customary manner. It will sit on this problem, wait until the parents grow weary, and then act against them. The Board can wait. It is never in any hurry to do anything in these areas.

• • •

THURSDAY
November 30

If only because today was payday, some teachers did manage a smile for one another. It is sad that politics can affect the feelings in a school so strongly. But the white teachers' fear of school decentralization is based on the fear that they will lose their jobs in the ghetto.

In the meantime the classes are suffering as teachers stand in doorways talking and politicking. Many are disturbed to the point where they attempt no teaching at all, only pupil assignments. The principal appears not to be aware of this split and has not called a meeting to discuss the growing tension, which many teachers feel should be done.

2
Winter

FRIDAY

December 1

The parents went down to Board of Education headquarters in Brooklyn in freezing weather to see the director of personnel and to demonstrate support for their candidate for principal. They came back with what appears on the surface to be a minor victory (a letter stating he will review the case). We shall have to wait and see.

The parents are so elated that they are having a champagne celebration party. Maybe now we can get down to the business of educating the children, who have suffered by the strike and now by this division of the teachers.

There appears to be an air of relief among the staff. Blacks and whites are glad the issue is resolved, even on the surface. One Negro teacher who has been teaching for fifteen years showed her joy with tears. "Whenever black people win anything from the Board, it is time for happy tears or shouts that things are changing," she exclaimed.

• • •

MONDAY

December 4

My fears have been proven correct. The parents have not really won. All they have is a sheet of paper promising to look into what they are demanding. They interpreted it incorrectly, and now they have to dig in for what will probably be a long fight. They have asked the superintendent of schools to give them a final decision by Thursday.

In the meantime, Arthur has been absent a week, Cherry is late constantly, and all the art materials are still in our classroom.

The guidance counselors are busy with the black-white

teacher split and have not been able to act on any of the pupil referral problems.

We had another false alarm today; apparently one or more pupils are having lots of fun in the midst of the chaos.

Everyone is back to business as usual—suspicion, hate, and fear, the hallmarks of education in the ghetto schools today.

• • •

TUESDAY

December 5

All the children brought money for Melvin's birthday party. We went shopping at a local supermarket for the goodies, using the shopping trip as a class lesson.

Melvin was unable to bring any money. It is usually a quarter from the child whose birthday we celebrate and ten cents each from the rest of the class. The day was very cold and some children did not have winter coats. They insisted on going with us and we allowed them to come after we found coats to fit them in the lost-and-found box in the office.

• • •

WEDNESDAY

December 6

A child was struck down by a truck during lunch hour. This is the first accident this term. Last April a boy was so badly injured that he was out of school the rest of the year. The boy who was hit today has multiple fractures and will be out for a long time.

There is still no playground for the children of our school. Last year the district superintendent promised that it would be completed at the start of this school year. The vacant lot next to the school is still not being worked on.

The children are still playing in the street, and a group of teachers formed a committee to protest to the local police precinct and to the Board of Education over the continued neglect of the playground project.

A few of us are hoping that this type of committee will also serve to bring more of the teachers back together into some kind of functioning unit.

• • •

THURSDAY

December 7

Cherry came to school today, but stayed in the girls' toilet all day—the second time she has done this. She wasn't discovered until afternoon, when a girl from our class saw her in the toilet.

I took her to the guidance counselor, whose first response was, "I think I had better call your mother." The girl is a foster child.

There are more problems with Alvin, the boy who is not officially on my register but sits in because he is a discipline problem. He's finally being sent to a new class, where he can get more help than I can give him. The guidance counselor decided that his mother should be the one to tell him. But Alvin came to school hostile and distressed over the change. He refused to go to the other class and is still sitting in with me.

• • •

FRIDAY

December 8

At first I thought Cherry hid in the toilet because she was afraid to come in late. But her attendance record indicates that she has not been on time since school started. There must be some other reason for her toilet refuge.

I took the problem to the guidance counselor again and the foster mother was called in. It seems that the child leaves home early enough to get to school on time, but always stops to talk to an older boy who does not attend school. I hope the mother can deal with this before it gets out of hand.

• • •

MONDAY
December 11

There still has been no decision on the principal's appointment. The parents are growing tired of this project and many have all but ended their activities; they have other immediate problems of their own. The Board is just sitting there.

The school has improved under the acting principal, but not the behavior of the children—they still carry on in the halls. They have torn down most of the Christmas bulletin-board presentations and decorations the classes have prepared for the holiday. Some teachers are concerned, but a great many just shake their heads instead of trying to keep their charges under control.

Many teachers, including me, did not put up bulletin boards this month because they would be torn down. Instead, I tacked a legend on the board: WATCH THIS SPACE FOR SOMETHING NEW AND DIFFERENT IN BULLETIN BOARDS.

• • •

TUESDAY
December 12

When it rains our school is a miserable place—as are most schools, I suppose. The children cannot go outside to play, and they are all over the halls, the auditorium, and the gym. Most teachers on duty do nothing about it; they are afraid to discipline the children because of the parents.

Many children stay home on rainy days because of bad shoes or insufficient clothing.

The bell is still not working, and the secretary again forgot to turn on the taped morning exercises. The principal got on the intercom and told us, "Please conduct your own morning exercises today."

• • •

THURSDAY
December 14

I was out yesterday with a bad cold.

Still no bell for the start of the day or for dismissal. The custodian does not seem to care.

The heat is on, but set at a very low temperature. This is a new school but it's cold in the classrooms. Perhaps if the broken windows were repaired it would not be so cold, especially in the halls and gym.

Wilbert told me today he wishes his mother would whip him because of something bad he did last night. I reported to the guidance counselor that Wilbert has extreme guilt feelings when he does something he should not have done and is not found out by his parents.

• • •

FRIDAY
December 15

This morning an irate mother started an argument with some teachers in the hall and cursed at the principal and the assistant principal. No one was able to reason with her.

The children stood in the hall listening to her foul language and cheering her on.

• • •

WEDNESDAY
December 20

This is my first day back after a bout with the flu. The teacher in charge while I was ill allowed the children to play all day, even though the plan book was in the desk drawer.

Our hamster was not fed or given water over the weekend and the two days I was out.

The Board still has not acted on the principalship. The bell still does not work and there was a false fire alarm this morning.

It seems as if I haven't been out at all. The old place is still the same. I don't know why I expected it to change. I suppose I was glad to be ill and stay out and have no guilt feelings about the school.

• • •

THURSDAY
December 21

There is general chaos in a school when a holiday approaches, but it's worse here.

The meeting of teachers yesterday to discuss the decentralization plan was a rehash of the fears of many that their jobs and their security will be lost if the community takes over control. None, however, seemed worried about the present state of education in this school or any of the others that are controlled by bureaucrats who have not been in a classroom in twenty years, and have never been in a ghetto school.

The bureaucrats almost never visit a Harlem school unless the press is around them to provide some publicity or the occasion is the dedication of a new school. They have lost any contact they may have had with the classroom.

Principals and assistant principals should teach at least one class a week to stay in touch with the needs of the children.

• • •

FRIDAY

December 22

TGIF, especially when it's the beginning of a long vacation, which many of us need so badly.

There were many parties in school today. Nothing much else going on, and teachers who did not have last-period classes left early.

A girl in the sixth grade composed the following Christmas poem, which was run off for the older classes.

A CHRISTMAS PRAYER

Oh, heavenly Father—
I pray and hope very hard
That our boys in Vietnam
Will return to their homes.
And that the boys who are ill
Will get better,
And let us have peace
Throughout the world
Forever.

Lord,
So many bad things are happening:
Hippies, drop-outs;
But I hope with the Lord's help
I will stay in school and become
A teacher, and a pianist.
God bless everybody everywhere, and
I hope everyone will have a wonderful and
Beautiful Christmas.

Amen!

• • •

TUESDAY
January 2

The first day back after the long holiday. Few children were present, due to an outbreak of flu that has hit the whole city. Those in school seemed glad to be back.

Fifteen teachers were absent. There is still a shortage of substitutes and many of us had to double up. Most teachers are reluctant to do so. It means a loss of preparation periods, which probably will not be made up. Besides, one class is difficult enough, but with two classes combined the trouble really starts. No teaching takes place, only a holding action until three o'clock.

• • •

WEDNESDAY
January 3

Very bad weather today. The children were not allowed to go outside and the result was added confusion.

A teacher received a threatening letter from a parent who promised to come down here and "thrash you good if you touch my child again." The teacher has never touched the pupil, although the child told her stepfather otherwise. The teacher has sent several notes to the parent to come in at his convenience to discuss the child's behavior, but he has not made an appearance so far.

• • •

THURSDAY

January 4

Parents who come in for help still get no assistance from the guidance personnel, both of whom are leaving next term for higher positions in the school system. They have a detached attitude about their work, now that they are about to leave. As a result, many of the services they usually give are not available.

Many teachers, growing tired of the situation here, are looking for jobs in other schools. Some expect to leave the system.

Neither the bell nor the broken windows have been repaired.

• • •

FRIDAY

January 5

It has been a long week, even though it was only four days. A notice that the School Day pictures are ready was sent around today. The names of the students who did not pay last year were attached. Phone numbers where the mothers can be reached are requested from these children.

Most of my students continue to come in late. "My mother slept late" run most of the excuses.

They don't usually have their homework. "My mother told me to shut up and watch TV when I asked her to help me" is a typical excuse. When I confront the parents they tell me they are too tired after work, even though I know many have no jobs.

Perhaps they mean "tired" from working at home, from struggling with three or four younger children, from trying to exist without money or opportunities. Many parents, however, do work, late into the night, and then come home to prepare meals.

The after-school study center is a good program. It provides a place to stay until five, when most parents get off work, and the children do not have to roam the streets.

• • •

MONDAY
January 8

Still having difficulty getting parents to see me about their children. Only one has shown up so far.

Today Wilbert's mother came in to discuss his retesting. He has been in CRMD for two years and should be retested, since his work and behavior have improved greatly. His younger brother in Junior Guidance* is to be tested for CRMD. His younger sister is in a regular class.

Most parents never visit the school unless their child has been in a fight. They almost never show up when the teacher sends for them.

Jesus's parents keep him out two to three times a week, the excuse usually being that he did not have a clean shirt. Yet he is one of the two children in the class whose families are not on welfare. Although he has an older brother and a younger sister, he is the only one of his family in a special class.

His brother has a sixty-six-year-old teacher with a reputation for being able to control difficult children. Of course no learning takes place there because she has to sit on them all day. She has them terrified.

Jesus stays out more than his sister or brother, and I have sent for his parents several times. I also keep trying to encourage him to clean up, but to no avail. I know what the problem is. In the winter ghetto children seldom have hot water or heat, so many sleep in their clothes. In the morning the house is so cold that they don't want to undress to put on clean clothes. Like most of the children in my class and in the school in general, Jesus wears dirty underclothing and seldom takes time to wash properly.

Most of the parents are too involved in trying to get sufficient money simply for food and to keep a roof over their heads to re-

*Special classes for disturbed and disruptive children.

member to wash their children. Many children in our school still wet their beds.

• • •

TUESDAY

January 9

The school was broken into early this morning—the fourth time since October. All the office rooms on the first floor and three classrooms were vandalized. There is broken window glass on the floors and in one classroom a pile of human waste. The intruders broke in through the gym doors, which had been used for an earlier break-in and had not been repaired.

There still are no burglar guards on the windows and the smashed-open doors are covered with makeshift pieces of plywood. The custodian insists that all he can do is take bids for the repairs and submit them to the Board. Getting a repair contract could take months.

• • •

WEDNESDAY

January 10

Attendance records of ghetto children in the dead of winter are unusually high. There is little or no heat at home and the parents get the children out early. Many of them are in school long before school officially opens and before the teachers arrive. The only exceptions in my class are the kids who ride buses.

There is a rash of tenement fires in our area every winter. There was a four-alarmer on the corner today. About thirty children were burned out in the three buildings that were on fire from ten to two o'clock. Our children could not go out to play because they might have impeded the firemen.

I started an experiment today—a "quiet hour" of music. We

just sit and listen to music of all kinds while we do our work. The music does not seem to affect the children's concentration as long as it is soft and low.

Teachers, black and white, and parents met today to discuss the Board's lack of action on our playground. We are still waiting for a response to long letters we sent before Christmas to the Board and to the district superintendent.

Cars still come through the school street on which one of the students suffered a serious accident last month.

• • •

THURSDAY

January 11

A parent came in today to see me because her son doesn't want me to "holler" at him. I had sent for her on several occasions, but she never came; she did not have time or her son did not give her the note. She has no telephone and I had to send repeated notes, since the mailbox in her building is always broken and she rarely gets her mail.

After she left I found a four-inch pocketknife on a string around the child's neck. He said his mother gave it to him because of the bigger boys in his neighborhood.

After I pursued the matter further he admitted, "Ma says if you touch me, to wait till you turn around and then stick you."

I sought one of the guidance officers, but she was not in her office, nor was the other to be found anywhere in the building, although they had come in to work this morning. We usually can't find them.

We had several severe cases of children vomiting during lunch, due to the flu virus.

• • •

FRIDAY
January 12

A teacher who left a day before the Christmas break returned today after an out-of-state trip. She has been out a lot, using up all her annual sick time in one term and taking advantage of the strike time and the Thanksgiving and Christmas holidays. The principal has not called her in about her absenteeism.

This is the same teacher the parents have complained about for wearing miniskirts. The boys sometimes let pencils fall in order to look up her dress. She does not pay any attention to this, and the parents have become alarmed. Many parents feel miniskirts in school are out of place. Her class has suffered a great deal on account of her absence, perhaps more so because it is a Junior Guidance class. She seems to have a good relationship with them, but the substitute had considerable difficulty.

• • •

MONDAY
January 15

The usual Monday-morning headaches. In addition, Melvin's little brother, who was in a foster home, died over the weekend. His mother came in and asked that Melvin be permitted to pay for his pictures later. Before I could say yes and express my sympathy, she had asked me to lend her some money until her next check. I did not have any, I explained.

Last year it was thought Melvin attempted to kill himself by setting fire to his apartment. The psychiatrist's report says he "has a subconcious desire to destroy himself." It turned out later that his mother may have set the fire. She was acquitted of the charge in court, but afterward she went around telling other parents in the neighborhood that she set the fire because she no longer wanted her children. She was reported to the authorities and it was determined that she had a long history of mental disorders and had been institutionalized.

• • •

TUESDAY

January 16

A boy in the fifth grade struck a teacher during gym. Although the boy is supposed to be very disturbed, teachers who were present say the incident was provoked by the teacher, whose previous experience has been in kindergarten and who is not satisfied with having an OTP assignment this year.

Later in the day a woman teacher was struck by the same boy. Nothing has been done about his obviously urgent psychological needs. His parents were not called in, nor has he been expelled—which might force the Bureau of Child Guidance to help him quickly.

These constant attacks on teachers by apparently disturbed children and the lack of support by supervisors create fear in many teachers of the impending school decentralization projects and the parents' role in such plans.

• • •

WEDNESDAY

January 17

There is difficulty with the music teacher, who does not feel that she should give music to the special classes, Junior Guidance and CRMD. She has been uncooperative, especially since she was told she will have to give music in the auditorium because her classroom is being turned over to the Afro-Arts cultural group.

One of the guidance people told me today that a fourth-grade teacher wants two disruptive boys to sit in my class.

According to my class records, Rachel, who is new in the class, should not be here. In her old school last year she scored grade level in all her subjects, but because she was shy and on occasions inattentive her teacher had her tested. The psychiatrist found her to be CRMD, even though she was on-level. I have reported all this to the principal and the guidance people, who have requested a retest.

• • •

THURSDAY
January 18

Another fight in the gym today, between the same gym instructor and a boy from the same class as on Tuesday. Again nothing was done. Something is wrong. The boys in that class feel they can pick on the gym teacher because nothing was done about the Tuesday incident. The teacher complains that he has to fend for himself; certainly no help is forthcoming from guidance or administration.

The older boys have discovered a new game. They urinate on the hot radiators in the lavatory. The odor is strong enough to turn the stomach.

• • •

FRIDAY
January 19

There was little cooperation in assembly today. Some teachers believe they should not insist on students wearing white shirts; others believe they should. It is the Board of Education's policy that students wear white shirts in assembly. Several teachers got into arguments over this. There was the usual friction over whether the children should be allowed to talk during assembly.

The two teachers who have the flag bearers in their class forgot to remind them to bring the flag, so at the flag pledging I had to stand on stage and hold a large flag which is normally used only for display. It is too heavy for any of the students.

The children regarded me as a very funny figure, standing there with the flag. They enjoyed seeing a teacher erect and immobile, looking like a complete nut. I enjoyed it too. At least it showed them that teachers can sometimes act foolish too, since they are always telling the kids how foolish they act.

• • •

MONDAY
January 22

The children in this school, as in most Central Harlem schools, are very hostile toward one another. They rarely engage in meaningful, organized play in the gym. They prefer tag and similar games in which physical contact is necessary. In most gym periods four or five fights will occur, especially when more than one class is participating.

Today was unusually tough in the gym, with seven fights breaking out over such charges as "he tagged me too hard" or "he pushed me instead of tagging me."

Two gym teachers supervise three to four classes three to four periods a day, and the going is usually pretty rough.

• • •

TUESDAY
January 23

Alvin, one of my former students who was sent to Junior Guidance, was running through the halls crying today. The principal sent me to calm him down. The trouble was that his teacher wanted to keep him in after three o'clock to finish his homework, but he had to go to the North Side Clinic.

Two Black Muslims entered the school today to see the principal, but not before they had cursed at three parent aides and attacked another.

The school clocks still have different times on each floor; the bell has not been fixed, and the playground has not yet been started. The children, parents, and teachers' committee are still writing letters to the Board and to the Mayor.

A typical communication by a third-grade student reads:

Dear Mayor Linsey,
   Please help us to get our playground field. One little boy has been hurt very badly already.

• • •

WEDNESDAY

January 24

It's time for the special classes to order materials for the next school year. Many of the things we order will not arrive, probably because they won't be in stock. If and when they do come, the term will be practically over.

Considerable food is being wasted in the dining area, but the dietician will not give extra portions even to the teachers who ask for them and even though the lunch charge has risen from fifty-five to seventy-five cents. We still receive the same amount as the kids. The quality of the food is terrible.

We still have not had a faculty meeting this year. But there is one scheduled for Monday. No doubt the supervisors will introduce the new staff. I would hope that by now the teachers know the new staff; we've been working with them since September.

• • •

THURSDAY

January 25

Wilbert's brother is to be examined today at Harlem Hospital. Their father has arrested t.b. and the brother is emotionally disturbed; he has been caught drinking water from the toilet bowls and the washbasins.

In March Rachel is going to be retested for re-placement. She should never have been placed in a CRMD class, according to departmental standards.

Wilbert is also going to be retested; he has been in CRMD for three years.

There are other children who, according to CRMD guidelines, should be retested, but this is being resisted by the counselors on the theory that these pupils are not ready. This is unfair to the students, who should be given every chance to move on to a regular class. Some would not make it, but they should be given the chance.

• • •

FRIDAY

January 26

I had lunch in the teachers' room today. The school lunches are so bad that I eat them only a few times a week. Most of the teachers were talking about trips they are planning for the spring break, decentralization issues, etc. Nothing new or very exciting.

A math teacher in her first year in a Harlem school was hit above the eye by a male pupil. This caused much discussion, particularly because the incident was not acted upon by the assistant principal in charge of her grade level.

There is trouble with several sixth-grade boys who are running an extortion game on the first- and second-graders. They are taking money on the promise to "beat up any other large guys who mess with" the youngsters. They have been taking money even from pupils in the special classes for disturbed children, which is easy picking because most of the other children do bother them.

• • •

MONDAY
January 29

Some older boys were caught molesting little girls. Everyone seems to be at a loss about what to do with this problem. A call was made to one boy's parents but not to the others.

The chairman of the teachers' social committee resigned to-day because of a dispute over five dollars of Christmas money, and the committee refused to give a farewell party for two staff members who are leaving.

We do not seem to be making any progress on the community-relations committees that several of us were so interested in starting. There is still an undercurrent of hate and bitterness among a great many of the staff.

The boys found taking money from the younger children were reprimanded and ordered to bring their parents in for conferences.

A teacher received a letter today from a black parent who stated that she did not want "no black teacher teaching my child."

• • •

TUESDAY
January 30

The music teacher has had to move to the third floor because the Afro-Arts Cultural Center has moved into her room. This has cre-ated even more problems than we expected. Noise in the halls, loss of teaching time, and breakage are always part of such moves.

There are protests from the first-grade teachers that they get no supervision from the assistant principal. The teachers say she hides from them.

Problems abound, with many forms of neurosis among the staff growing out of feelings of pity and sorrow for the children.

A male teacher was caught "petting" a first-grade girl. He was relieved of his kindergarten class and given a cluster assignment. But a lot of pressure is being brought on him and he will not be back next year. Black teachers are in a rage because he is white. The incident probably will not go into his record, and he'll go on to some other school.

• • •

WEDNESDAY
January 31

Tomorrow marks the beginning of the new term. Many teachers are leaving, including one assistant principal who only two days ago revealed her decision. Things appear to be falling apart.

There are between one and two thousand books that are to go on our library shelves, but the librarian has not been able to put them up. Most of them have been on the floor since school started.

Over five hundred letters informing parents that they can attend evening classes for basic English and math were sent out. Only fifteen responded. One mother sent the letter back unopened. Many, many more need these classes, as evidenced by letters from parents:

> Dear Mr. Askis,
> Melvin was so ick that I get home.
> Mrs. Annie

> Dear Mr. Haskins,
> Joe had to stay home yesterday because he had tomarch ach. Thank you.
> Mrs. Johnson

• • •

THURSDAY
February 1

Cherry's mother kept her out of school today to take her to the optometrist, in spite of at least ten notes advising her to take the child to an eye specialist. Cherry did come to school this morning, but only to bring in her little cousin her mother takes care of.

I am still after Jesus to comb his hair. He is Puerto Rican and therefore different from the other children in color and hair texture. He says he is white and all he has to do is put water on his hair.

I have explained to him that he is Puerto Rican and that some Puerto Ricans are white and others are black, but Puerto Ricans on the whole are a mixture of black and white, and at any rate, everyone should comb his hair, no matter what color he is.

• • •

FRIDAY
February 2

Here is a pupil's letter to an absent teacher, which is just about the only good thing to happen today:

Dear Miss Henry,

I am very sorry that you were not able to come to school today; however, from now on I am going to control myself and do my work and when I get finish I will let you check my work and when you finish checking it I will read a book. And also I hope you will keep your confidence in me. I really hope you will be able to come back tomorrow. (I have faith in you and confidence in you even if you scream at me I still love you.) I hope that you will get better by tomorrow.

Sincerely yours,
Betty Jones

• • •

MONDAY
February 5

Today I received a postcard from my CRMD supervisor at headquarters in Brooklyn; he must be a very busy man because, while
the card was properly addressed, there was no message on the
back. I will never find out what the intended message was, since
only the resource teacher is allowed to call him and she refuses
to. She insists that I should mail it back to embarrass him, but
he'd probably never get it in the maze of bureaucracy that is the
Board of Education.

A thirteen-year-old student in the school down the street was
found shot to death this morning. He had not been seen or heard
from all the previous day. His parents did not worry about him
until late last night since it was his habit to stay out after his paper route was finished on Sunday.

A female teacher who usually has coffee with me before
school starts told me that right across the street from the school,
and in full view of at least twenty classrooms, we have an exhibitionist. He stands in front of his window and exposes himself.

When I expressed surprise she shrugged and said, "We have
another one down the street." She couldn't recall whether or not
the police had ever been called. Her exhibitionist has been at it
the three years she has been here.

We reported the matter to the assistant principal, who called
the police.

• • •

TUESDAY

February 6

Joe came to school today with soap in his hair. He explained that he had washed his hair last night but the soap would not come out this morning when he used his comb.

The bells were fixed today, after being out of order since last term. The playground construction was finally started, too. Both on the same day!

The morale of the teachers continues to decline. Today a fourth-grade student told a white substitute teacher, "Keep your damn hands off me!" when she touched him on the shoulder and requested him to sit down.

This particular class has a black militant teacher who hates whites with a passion that inevitably rubs off on the children. She openly flaunts her hatred and contempt for whites, even in staff meetings. When she is out, the children give any white substitute a hard time.

• • •

WEDNESDAY

February 7

This morning I discussed the exhibitionist problem with the new guidance counselor.

The assembly program was especially good today. James Meredith was the guest speaker and he gave an exceptional talk on the problems that confront the Negro. He spoke in language the children could understand.

A false fire alarm at the end of assembly sent all the children scurrying out into the cold without coats, since we had left them in our rooms.

Most of my children have speech problems. The speech teacher from the CRMD bureau comes once a week. She will start in a new school this term and last week was her final visit with us. She was very good with the children and we shall miss her.

• • •

THURSDAY

February 8

Cherry brought another letter from the Seventh Avenue optometrist saying that she doesn't need glasses. I keep advising Cherry's foster mother to take her to a specialist because even in the front row the child cannot see the work on the blackboard.

Narcotics are being sold on the street right below our window. Many of the school's supportive staff play the numbers in front of the children. This is common knowledge and the practice is generally accepted; no one says anything to upset the status quo.

• • •

FRIDAY

February 9

I reported to the assistant principal that the exhibitionist was in his window again today. A policeman interviewed me this afternoon and promised to have a plainclothesman in the school today and from Monday on.

The citywide sanitation strike has begun to affect this street. The first few days it didn't matter much because this block is usually filthy, but now it's even worse.

Some children reported that they can't sleep at night because "the rats make so much noise." Walking to school this morning, I saw a large one running from a huge pile of trash and garbage into a tenement.

• • •

MONDAY

February 12

The plainclothesman did not show up this morning and the exhibitionist across the street executed his daily routine.

Sidney came to class this morning very sleepy and nervous; he said he got a whipping for nothing last night. He says he always gets whipped for no reason ever since 1965, when he broke one of his mother's favorite statues. (What is the significance of his remembering the date?)

On cold days we can see from our windows the older people sitting bundled in coats and scarves inside the poorly heated apartments. On the street the steady stream of welfare workers and public health nurses go about their usual routines.

● ● ●

TUESDAY

February 13

Almost every Tuesday, which is fifth- and sixth-grade assembly day, I get some sixth-graders who are not wearing white shirts and therefore cannot go to assembly. I received two today from a class of "disruptive" boys.

Joe's mother came in today to ask if I knew where she could call to get some heat in her apartment. I referred her to the Guidance Department. Later in the day I saw the new guidance counselor, who expressed his lack of interest in handling "this kind of thing" and said he would talk to me later to "define" his "duties."

Melvin's mother brought him to school at eleven today. They had to walk because she had no money and he did not have a bus pass. They live only fifteen blocks from school, straight up Eighth Avenue. Every month Melvin receives a free bus pass, which he promptly manages to lose; most of the bus drivers know him, however, and would ride him for free, as he knows.

When his mother left, I questioned him and learned that he and his mother had slept late, and that he sleeps with his mother even though they have five rooms. Sometimes they "just lie in bed and play." I referred the information to my resource teacher and I suppose the guidance people will take up the matter.

• • •

WEDNESDAY
February 14

I received a letter today from Wilbert's mother, one of the few parents who is alert and really aware of her three schoolchildren's difficulties.

> Dear Mr. Haskins,
>
> Here is an excuse for Wilbert to go to the Dentist. Hope Wilbert is doing OK. Will see you soon. They have a new teacher for Willie. I'm giving her a try. Because Mrs. Brown was no good for him and Miss Young would not place him anywhere else. But if this teacher doesn't help him I have a surprise for Miss Young and the Guidance Department. Will tell you about it when I see you.
>
> Mrs. Williams.

There were two incidents today involving the music teacher. In one sixth-grade class she grabbed a child to emphasize her point and was kicked in the stomach. Instead of cooling off she attempted to teach another class; this time she was bitten on the arm and was taken to Harlem Hospital for a tetanus shot.

The water fountain broke in the room across the hall from me. Classes had to be evacuated because the water spilled over into several classrooms before it was shut off.

• • •

THURSDAY
February 15

The first thing this morning a teacher across the hall allowed two boys to fight in full view of the class. After he thought they had fought it out, he intervened and punched both of them for fighting.

One class put on a superb performance at assembly today in celebration of Negro History Week. Very informative. When the teacher asked who Nat Turner was, a boy answered, "He led a rebellion to get whitey," causing a stir among some white teachers.

The parent aides are an ineffective group. Apparently they are kept on because some of them are officials or ex-officials of the parents' organization. Some do not have children in school, so the term parent aide is a misnomer. They are having their own internal strife over a new aide who is much younger and prettier. Many are old and can't keep up with the children, who are constantly doing things to them and running away knowing they can't be caught.

A new teacher has taken over as social committee chairman and it has been decided that henceforth parents from the community will be invited to participate in teacher social gatherings.

The swinging doors on the third floor are jammed and open only one way. A teacher tried to go through them this morning and was hurt. The doors have been out of order since yesterday, but the custodian has not even posted warning signs.

The windows still have not been fixed, and there is still no progress in getting the dietitian to serve more food to teachers or even to discuss it reasonably. And still the parent preoccupation with the Junior Guidance teacher's miniskirt.

Another Junior Guidance teacher, who couldn't control her class, has been relieved and made a cluster teacher.

A new program has been started for volunteers from Harlem Prep° to assist some teachers in the language arts. At least one teacher has already expressed serious doubts concerning the project.

Melvin had a ten-o'clock appointment with the guidance counselor, but when I took him to the office the counselor was not ready to see him. The counselor did not see Melvin at all today.

Wilbert had a fire in his building this morning and didn't come to school.

The former president of our PTA was burned out last week. There was a collection for her and the two children. She is eight months pregnant.

• • •

FRIDAY

February 16

The detective in charge of the exhibitionist incident called today for further information. I had already reported all I knew to the local police precinct.

The music teacher went back to the doctor today. She has a blood clot as a result of the bite she received Wednesday trying to stop a fight between a girl and a boy in a sixth-year class. When she reached out to part them, the little girl bit her.

We had a guest from Thailand today. She exhibited jewelry and clothing from her country and gave the children picture post-cards of Thailand. During the question-and-answer period Joe asked her what was the zip code of her country, in case he wanted to send her a card. She did not understand, and when I explained what the zip code system was, she laughed and told the class that zip codes were not needed there because her country was much smaller than the United States.

°A new private high school for dropouts, the only high school in Central Harlem.

. . .

MONDAY
February 19

We received a memo today on corporal punishment:

> The superintendent wants to remind all teachers that Section 90 of the Board of Education bylaws states: "No corporal punishment shall be inflicted in the public schools nor any kind tending to cause excessive fear or physical or mental distress." Principals must impress the faculty with the importance of observing this bylaw.

The fourth-grade teacher who hates whites lost her white student teacher from Bank Street today because the supervisor felt that the student teacher "could not function in a black-power-type placement." The teacher's immediate response was, "What they are both missing is the fact that when she starts teaching, chances are she'll be teaching in one."

A boy insisted on going through the broken swinging door on the third floor today. A teacher cautioned him and he suddenly let go of the door. It struck her on the hand, which at the end of the day was badly bruised and swollen.

The custodian, who is white, has been very negligent in repairing many of the things in need of repair, using the excuse that he has to get "estimates and okays on all repairs." This is not exactly true for things like doors and broken windows. What he doesn't say is the fact that he tries to get the lowest estimates on all repairs, for whatever he can save in repair bills goes into his pocket. Custodians operate on budgets and they have the last say on prices. Ours spends three or four weeks looking for the lowest bidder in order to save money. Custodians make more money than a principal and two teachers combined; some make as high as $40,000 a year.

• • •

TUESDAY
February 20

The injured teacher's hand is black and blue this morning. She is a three-year veteran of teaching in Harlem schools and is now thinking of trying a new "adventure."

I began an experiment with the sixth grade's best readers. They will come to us once a week for forty-five minutes to help my children learn to read.

One of the science teachers told this story today in the teachers' room: He was explaining to his class that everything that goes up must come down. One boy frowned, raised his hand, and said, "But teacher, that's not true."

The teacher asked, "Why not?"

The boy responded, "My age. My age goes up and never comes down."

• • •

WEDNESDAY
February 21

Today was especially chaotic. It was five degrees this morning. A lot of teachers were out, and it was very difficult getting substitutes. In one class a little girl threw a chair, hitting the substitute on the leg. The sub swears she'll never come to this school again.

The detective has not yet been in to observe the man across the street, who is still exhibiting himself.

The principal was looking for one of the new guidance counselors all day, only to discover that he had gone to the Malcolm X celebration at IS 201.

From the window it was the usual news—the numbers runners and the drug sellers.

The principal called at two-fifteen to ask another male teacher and me to break up a fight in the black-power advocate's class. Two boys there are constantly fighting and should be put into separate classes.

· · ·

FRIDAY
February 23

A lot of teachers were absent today, many making a long weekend out of yesterday's Washington's birthday holiday.

One of the white cluster teachers, the one who was relieved of his kindergarten assignment, asked two girls to take his shoes to his official room and bring back his old pair. Each girl carried one shoe. Until they returned, he stood with no shoes on in the classroom in full view of the thirty-three children. This teacher often comes to school with his face unwashed and his pajamas on under his pants.

I went to our library this morning to pick up some books the district library coordinator said we had. They were not available; still piled on the floor and not yet catalogued.

Another pupil was hit by a car today on 134th Street. One of the parent aides moved the boy before the ambulance arrived. She says she didn't know she was not supposed to move him while he was lying in the street. We could not tell whether the boy was further injured by the moving, since he was already unconscious.

· · ·

MONDAY
February 26

Still no detective to check on the man who continues to exhibit himself before the window.

One of the special teachers is still out. He went to the week-long carnival in the West Indies.

The boys from Harlem Prep, who have volunteered their services in reading, make it a habit to smoke in the halls. No one seems to mind. I spoke to the guidance counselor about it, but he said it was okay since they were on their way out of the buildings.

A student was sent to the office on a probable suspension; he was caught burning a desk in the back of the room.

A faculty meeting today could not resolve any of the problems in the school. It ended up in a loud exchange of open hostilities between several white and black teachers who have been carrying on a constant dialogue of hate.

• • •

TUESDAY

February 27

Still a good many teachers out today.

I broke up two fights in the next room. The regular teacher was out and the substitute couldn't handle the class. This teacher is out a lot and the class practically never does any work for the few substitutes who do try to teach. This is a sixth-grade class that is expected to go on to junior high school next year.

Most of the classes are already two to three years behind in reading, and they fall even further behind in all subject areas as a result of teacher absenteeism. However, this has been commonplace in their whole school experience.

• • •

WEDNESDAY

Februry 28

There were so many children running around in the halls today that it looked like some kind of celebration.

The music teacher gave no music to the special classes.

The third-floor doors are still not fixed. The children play with them all day.

I had lunch away from the school today with a white woman teacher. The guidance counselor came over to our table and remarked, "If I ever saw you lunching with a Negro woman I guess I'd faint." He is black.

The teacher seemed very upset about his statement. According to school gossip, she knows him better than I.

• • •

THURSDAY

February 29

Melvin was absent and his mother came in this morning looking for him. She said she sent him to school, but I know she didn't because he's been staying with his aunt since last Friday. His mother said she'll "kill" him when she finds him.

Lena's mother finally had the child's glasses fixed, but they have new temple pieces which do not match the rest of the glasses. Minimal commercial decency would have made the man provide matching temples, especially since both were broken.

I had been sending notes to Lena's mother for several weeks, asking her to have the glasses fixed since the child could not see without them. She had taken to leaving them at home because the children laughed at her for wearing glasses with only one temple piece.

3
Spring

FRIDAY

March 1

So many teachers were out today that the principal asked me to take charge of a sixth-grade class no one else would take. My children were put in with another CRMD class.

One very disturbed sixth-grade boy refused to go to his math class because the teacher was white. He stood in the hall and shouted insults at both the math teacher and me. The parent aide would not go get anyone from the guidance office. She said she had been down several times about this boy already.

Melvin's mother came looking for him again this morning. I referred her to the guidance office.

My class was observed by the assistant principal in charge of my grade today.

After I taught a language-art class (we did some original poems), the observer said the lesson was very good but there were two things wrong—there was no card with my name on the door and there was some paper on the floor in the back of the room.

• • •

MONDAY

March 4

Cherry got her new glasses today. She says she can see much better now. I have been trying to get her a correct prescription since last year.

Melvin came to school today. He told me he had spent the last two days working in a laundry because he didn't want to go to school. His mother had sent him to stay with his aunt while her boyfriend was visiting, and he decided to take off when his mother would not be around to check on him.

I caught the exhibitionist doing his thing again today. The police still have not sent a detective to check on him.

Twice a year the teachers have to give each student an eye, height, and weight examination and report the information on the student's health card. Many teachers believe that a day is lost doing this; besides, none of us feels competent to give eye exams, the bathroom scales we use to weigh the children are usually inaccurate, and measuring height with a yardstick is wholly inadequate.

• • •

TUESDAY

March 5

There was a large fire on 133rd Street today. Five families lost their homes and all their possessions. Only two students from our school lived in the building.

There's trouble between the custodian and his men. He wants to fire one man, but the other two say they too will have to be fired if he does. In the meantime every clock in the school still has a different time; the doors on the third floor have not been fixed; all the doors need oiling; the floors are half-swept and the classrooms half-cleaned.

Today a substitute teacher in the first grade discovered as she was leaving that her purse with three twenty-dollar bills was missing. She returned to the school to find a little boy in the hall with her purse. He thought the bills were play money because they were twenties. She recovered two of the bills, but had given one to another boy, who could not be found at his home.

The guidance counselor checked the neighborhood and found a storekeeper who had thought it strange for a kid that age to have a twenty and took it from him. The storekeeper turned it over to the guidance counselor who, in turn, brought it to the principal, who put it on her desk.

Then a fight broke out in the hall, and when the guidance counselor and the principal returned to the office they discovered that the twenty was missing.

• • •

WEDNESDAY
March 6

Another fire today, on Eighth Avenue. No one was hurt and no children from our school were left homeless. However, the children's lunchtime play was restricted because of the fire engines in the street. They are still building the playground, but all we can see are holes.

The music teacher was among several other teachers out today, so again no music for our class. It seems she's always out, and when she's here she's so busy that we rarely get music these days.

The school seemed very lonely today, but this is not unusual when a lot of teachers are absent, as they have been recently.

There are many good teachers in this school, but there are more bad than good ones. One teacher has taught here for twenty-five years and her pupils attest to her dedication—for the most part they are well-grounded in their basic skills. On the other hand, there are fifth- and sixth-grade students who do not know their ABCs.

• • •

THURSDAY
March 7

A parent aide was hit today by the same boy who cursed me out last week. This pupil was recently released from the state mental hospital, but apparently he is still not well. He should be receiving help from the guidance office.

Cherry left her glasses at home today. She says her mother forgot to give them to her.

There was a fight between two girls in the sixth grade and they were sent to Harlem Hospital for treatment. Fights among students are an integral part of the daily activities here. The number of fights grows during the latter part of the week. The children tend to "get" one another for acts committed on Monday or Tuesday. Generally nothing is done except to try to break them up, although the more serious ones do receive some attention. The Guidance Department is overloaded with other problems.

• • •

FRIDAY
March 8

Cherry has lost her glasses and does not know where she may have left them. I sent her to the general office to see if they were reported lost.

The fifth- and sixth-year Iowa Reading scores came back today. Most of our fifth- and sixth-grade pupils are on the fourth-year level, many lower, and some are down to the second-year level.

I had to break up two fights in a class whose regular teacher was absent because of illness.

A sixth-grade girl took the math teacher for a quarter during lunch hour the other day. The child walked into the teachers' room and asked for the quarter she said she had given the teacher for safekeeping that morning. The teacher could not remember the girl's giving her any money, but since it was a possibility, she gave her a quarter.

After lunch she asked the other children whether they remembered the girl's approaching her during the morning. They said no.

She then prevailed upon the girl to tell the truth; she admitted that she had not given the teacher a quarter to hold.

The incident was reported to the mother, who wrote back, "Here's your old quarter."

This girl does something every day that suggests she needs help, which she is not receiving.

• • •

MONDAY
March 11

Someone took our hamster over the weekend. When I came to school this morning he was gone. We looked everywhere, but he was not to be found.

No real difficulties today other than the usual gloomy outlook on the Iowa scores.

I saw the exhibitionist at the window again this morning. Still no action by the police.

Cherry arrived late, as usual. Her excuse is her mother's— "She had to brush her teeth." She still has not found her glasses.

Melvin came to school without his books. He said he had not been home because he and his mother had stayed with their friend over the weekend. He means his mother's boyfriend.

Sometimes she takes Melvin with her; other times she either leaves him alone or takes him over to his great-aunt, who is an alcoholic and a hypochondriac.

• • •

TUESDAY
March 12

A lot of teacher absenteeism today. The children in Junior Guidance were constantly in the hall; their substitute was one they'd never had before. They were joined by children who walked out of the math class.

Whoever stole our hamster must have returned it after school yesterday. We found it back in its cage this morning.

A boy in another class was unable to hold his bowels until he got to the bathroom. The whole class was disrupted. The teacher had to clean up the mess because it took so long for the custodial help to arrive.

• • •

WEDNESDAY
March 13

An argument between two sixth-grade teachers over a spelling bee broke out in the assembly in front of all the children. The teacher whose class did not win felt it should have because her pupils had higher spelling scores on the Iowa tests.

A little girl went to the principal this morning with a complaint that one of the parent aides had taken twenty dollars from her. By lunch time she admitted that she had made it all up, and we gave up looking for a parent aide "in a black-and-white dress" and breathed a sigh of relief.

• • •

THURSDAY
March 14

The fourth- and fifth-year classes had visitors from PS 108 who presented a good program in the auditorium on African history and black personalities.

The custodian is still causing a lot of trouble trying to get rid of one of his workers. Now he is holding up the man's check.

The fire alarm rang again today, and before the principal could announce that it was a false alarm, many classes donned hats and coats and made for the street. Some classes did not respond at all.

• • •

FRIDAY
March 15

The two sixth-grade teachers are still at each other's throats. The grade meeting to resolve the matter didn't help and the principal has taken no action.

There's chaos in the school, with teachers staying out four and five days at a time. The miniskirted Junior Guidance teacher, who stayed an extra week abroad during the holidays, has been out all week.

Cherry's foster mother came in today with a sob story to get a free pair of glasses for her daughter. I had just sent her all the information for obtaining free glasses, but she says she misplaced it. She may be hiding the "lost" glasses because she feels Cherry does not need them.

Everybody in school knows Cherry's mother. She keeps children for working parents and is in school many times during the day to pick them up.

• • •

MONDAY
March 18

The custodian met with the union delegate today. It was revealed that one of the custodial workers was writing numbers. The police came and the worker ran away. But the incident is causing more dissent among the custodial help.

The doors on the third floor are still not repaired. Running away from two other boys in the hall, a little boy slammed into the door and received a large bump on his forehead. He refused to go to the nurse.

• • •

TUESDAY
March 19

The psychologist visited the school today to retest Wilbert. After the interview she reported that the boy has a good chance for regular class placement.

Rachel still hasn't been retested.

Two fights between sixth-grade boys today. The substitute could not break them up.

A parent came in to see about her son at the request of the assistant principal. She started shouting at him for allowing her son to remain in the class where he repeatedly gets into trouble with the same boy.

The assistant principal said nothing; he just stood there shaking his head and writing something in his little black book.

• • •

WEDNESDAY
March 20

Everybody knew the principal was out of school all day for a meeting and the students went wild, while most of the teachers stood talking in the halls.

Many teachers admit that the school is really controlled by the students. They call it "the snake pit" or "the ship of fools" because so many teachers appear on the edge of a mental breakdown. About four teachers who have been "released from duties" at other schools have found a home here.

The mother of a fifth-grade boy came in at the request of the teacher, who told her that the boy's work was inferior to his capacity to achieve. The mother showed the teacher four previous assignments all marked excellent by the teacher and asked how that could be. When the teacher looked further, she found that it was the boy's own writing.

• • •

THURSDAY
March 21

The exhibitionist is still in his window. Nothing has been done about him yet.

Lena came to school with a new pair of glasses.

Cherry's mother came in again to see about the child's glasses.

School is in a general state of disarray. Someone pulled the fire alarm again today. This happens two or three times a week.

The principal tries to find out which children were out of the rooms when there is a false alarm. This never works because there are always some teachers who are out of their rooms at the same time.

• • •

FRIDAY
March 22

Irene took fifty cents from Cherry while we were out of the room. I wrote notes to the parents of both children.

The guidance counselor left today to become an assistant principal at IS 201. Now we have only one person in Guidance.

Report cards for the school were given out today and the teachers expect a flood of parents on Monday, all dissatisfied with the reports.

Helen told me she has six younger brothers and sisters. She's ten years old and has to help her mother clean up and wash dishes, so she does not have time to do her homework.

After we talked about her problem I told her that I would give her less homework in the future. She smiled and walked back to her seat as if a great load had been taken off her shoulders.

• • •

MONDAY
March 25

Cherry came to school with the same glasses she had said were lost. Probably when the mother saw her report card she "found" the glasses on the assumption that they would help Cherry get better grades.

I sent notes to the parents today, asking them to come in to discuss their children. I do not expect many of them to show up.

Sidney told me there was a fire in his apartment last night because his mother was smoking in bed.

Another false fire alarm today. No one budges now when the alarm is sounded.

• • •

TUESDAY
March 26

Lena's mother came in today, very angry with her daughter because she received three unsatisfactories, one in self-control. She wanted to whip her in front of the class!

She was also angry because she felt I was persecuting the child. She said she had not received the five or six notes I had sent her about Lena's behavior. Lena admitted that she had thrown them away. The mother warned her daughter, in front of the class, that she would "kill" her when she got her home.

After her mother left, Lena began to cry. I told her I'd write a note asking her mother not to whip her if she promised to give it to her. She promised.

• • •

WEDNESDAY
March 27

Lena told me that her mother whipped her "pretty bad" last night and made her go to bed without any food.

I received a response on the parent's comment section of a report card: "This child should be taken off retarded class and put in a regular class. His I.Q. is above the class he is in. He needs to meet competition."

This parent has been to see me only once and that was when the child lied that I would hit him when he did not have his homework.

Irene brought a note from her mother: "Please excuse this girl for March 25 and 26. She is sick."

Kenny was transferred to my class today; his teacher caught him molesting a little girl. The teacher was unable to cope with this kind of behavior but did not refer the boy for help. I reported the incident to Guidance.

• • •

THURSDAY
March 28

Melvin's mother brought him to school because he did not have his homework. She told me again that she has only a third-grade education and therefore can't help him with it. She admonished me to teach him more than he's learning. I told her she must be responsible for his homework habits.

Someone pulled the fire alarm again.

We found four-letter words in red paint on the walls in the boys' room on the first floor.

• • •

FRIDAY
March 29

Wilbert has the measles. I received a note from his mother this morning:

> Dear Mr. Haskins:
>   Wilbert has a lot of pimples on his face and body. I dont know if he has the measles or not. But any way am calling the doctor. And if he says he can come back to school, will send him tomorrow. Keep well. Will see you soon. Freddie has his homework. If he has any for today send it by Freddie.
> Thanks
Mrs. Williams

> P.S. Oh! Please send his report back so I can sign it. Wilbert took it back before I could sign it and write the remarks.

Cherry's mother brought her to school this morning, with her math homework that someone else did but did not explain to her. Several fights today among the fourth- and fifth-year children. Some fifth-year boys opened all the windows on the third floor. It was great weather outside but the hallways got drafty. The parent aide on the floor asked the boys to close the windows, but her pleas went unheeded. She reported them to the principal.

• • •

MONDAY
April 1

April Fool's Day—the children were in a festive mood trying to "April fool" the teachers. And many cases of false fire alarms.
    There's growing trouble in the sixth grade. A female teacher

who has not had a regular class for about eighteen years has taken over the class of a male teacher who was moved to Guidance to replace the counselor who left to go to IS 201. It is a tough class. The other sixth-year teachers doubt if the new teacher is adequate for the job.

Most classes are taking the Metropolitan Reading Tests this week. Everybody is hoping for better than last year's scores.

The new boy, Kenny, has been to school only once since he was transferred. He does not like the rule that he can't run all over my classroom.

Wilbert's mother sent him back to school today. The school doctor checked him and decided it was just a rash, not measles.

Irene's mother has not responded to the official letter concerning her daughter's behavior.

• • •

TUESDAY

April 2

Melvin has not been to school since Thursday. A series of 407's° has been sent out on him but no response is expected for about a week. He may be back by then, with some fantastic story about why he has been absent so long.

Like most students in this school, Melvin has no telephone or emergency number. Even parents with phones rarely call to report absences, and in most cases when the child does return to school, he's just back, with no excuse from the parent.

Some of the children reported that they had seen Melvin at the local bathhouse, where the children swim. Others said they saw him carrying packages at a supermarket.

Irene's mother was supposed to come in today, but Irene didn't think she'd show up because she was still in bed when

°A chronic absenteeism form sent to the attendance teacher, formerly the truant officer.

Irene left this morning. Her mother has no phone either. When she didn't keep the appointment, we tried the emergency number she had given me, but it's a pay phone in a candy store and no one seems to know her there.

$$\bullet \quad \bullet \quad \bullet$$

WEDNESDAY
April 3

Our man was in the window again this morning. It was reported to the assistant principal, who again called the police station. They said they will send a patrolman today.

The police, however, are in the school every day about thefts from Woolworth's or other local stores. Our children engage in these petty thefts during lunchtime.

Today a little boy just missed being hanged playing cowboys and Indians. About five boys tied his hands behind his back, roped his neck, threw the loop around the staircase railing, and began pulling him off the floor. He started to yell and was inches off the floor before some teachers heard him and stopped the "game."

$$\bullet \quad \bullet \quad \bullet$$

THURSDAY
April 4

Spring seems to bring indoor graffiti with it. On the wall of the gym in large black-ink lettering is CHARLIE BROWN IS A PUNK, signed by HIS BEST FRIEND. Another, in the third-floor boys' room, is DOWN WITH WHITEY.

The kindergarten's pet guinea pig, Joey, got hold of some poison when the exterminator was here Monday, and is quite sick. The children in the class are very upset about it.

There was a rash of paper-clip shooting today. One boy has a large welt where he was hit under the eye. A fifth-year girl was shot in the leg, and while the clip was still sticking in her calf, ran out in the hall crying loudly.

• • •

FRIDAY
April 5

The death of the Reverend Martin Luther King has shaken the school. Rioting in our neighborhood kept many children at home. Many white teachers were afraid to come to school today. The children and teachers who were here were heartsick. No one wanted to do any work.

There were four false fire alarms today. Most of them occur during the lunch hour, when many junior high boys come to the building either to take their sisters and brothers home for some extra lunch or just to hang around and pull the alarm to frighten half the school to death.

Kenny still has not been to school. I called his aunt, who said his mother hasn't been home to send him off to school, and besides, she said, "he has no shoes."

• • •

MONDAY
April 8

Melvin's mother brought him to school today. She said he had been ill with a virus but she hadn't take him to a doctor.

Kenny came in this morning, but without books, pencils, or papers. His aunt is responsible for him until his mother decides to come home. His mother often goes away and none of the family, including Kenny, seems to be upset by it.

Tomorrow all schools will be closed for Dr. King's funeral.

• • •

WEDNESDAY
April 10

Our class made a trip to the Bronx Zoo today. Jesus's mother did not dress him properly, but we took him anyway. He wore a ragged, filthy brown coat, a brown sock on one foot, a blue one on the other.

The children were very excited and had a good time. Sidney was lost for a while, but he finally found us over at the monkey house. Wilbert didn't bring any money and I had to give him ten cents for milk. The cheese sandwiches prepared by the school were without butter or mayonnaise, but an apple was included in each lunch.

General Staff Bulletin No. 16, received today, includes these regulations:

> In view of the general unrest occasioned by the many happenings which created tension, may I ask that no parties be held. This includes the "surprise" parties which the children like to give their teachers.
>
> Since the spring vacation is used for cleaning the rooms, please make sure that your room is left in the condition which will make this general cleaning easier for the staff. Kindly remove all materials from the window ledges and have the floors free of all boxes, bundles, etc. Despite my constant pleas, many rooms are not kept in the kind of order which denotes professionalism.
>
> If you have in your room equipment such as the overhead projector, record players, tape recorders, etc., please make sure that they are left in a safe place where they will not be stolen or where they will not be knocked over and broken. We have to take care of our equipment since we are sure that there will be no replacement when this initial allotment of audio-visual supplies is exhausted.

• • •

THURSDAY
April 11

I received a note from Joe's mother today:

> Dear Mr. Haskins:
>   Joe did not come into school Wednesday because He Had Toothache. Thank You.
>
>   Mrs. T.B. Johnson

The children are looking forward to the Easter break, April 12 through April 21.

A few false fire alarms today. They never seem to catch the culprits.

• • •

MONDAY
April 22

Our first day back. Many teachers are absent, but all my students are back, most of them in new clothes and shoes. They all said they had an enjoyable vacation.

Hal didn't get anything, he reported, but his mother got his brother a new suit.

Wilbert said he "only got a new pair of socks."

There was a false fire alarm today while visitors were in the school. They started to react to the alarm before it was announced over the p.a. system that the alarm was false.

• • •

THURSDAY
April 23

We visited the Aquarium, in Brooklyn, with three other classes. One class acted very badly. The teacher doesn't attempt to control the bad habits of his children. He believes in total permissiveness, and it shows whenever we go on trips together. His charges usually succeed in embarrassing the rest of us, running away from him and using foul language. One boy kept throwing rocks at the Aquarium's new killer whale.

• • •

WEDNESDAY
April 24

We had a false alarm at lunch today while three classes from Nathan Hale Junior High School were visiting the Afro-Arts Cultural Center. This time the boy was caught.

Kenny cheated on the spelling quiz today. After I called out the first word, he went ahead and wrote the second word on the spelling list. He was copying the words directly from the study list.

Wilbert was also caught cheating on the test. I have sent for both parents.

• • •

THURSDAY
April 25

A boy created a disturbance in the joint assembly today while we were being entertained by the Young Audiences, a music group, and the teacher asked him to leave. On his way out he encountered the principal, who apparently did not know he had been dismissed by his teacher, and she ordered him back to his seat.

The boy pulled away from the principal and ran between the rows of seated children, screaming, "Get your damn hands off of me, get your damn hands off of me!"

Children began shouting, "Play some jazz," over the strains of the selected songs on the program. Most of the assembly joined in. The principal was busy with the boy and the assistant principal stood in shocked amazement. One teacher who tried to stop the outburst was told by a black teacher that this was not his assembly and that his class was only an invited guest. Finally the Young Audiences halted their concert and left the assembly. The rest of the children were kept in the auditorium and given a talk about their behavior.

• • •

FRIDAY
April 26

The teacher's relationship with the boy involved in yesterday's incident has some of the aspects of a fight between wife and husband, with the wife—the teacher—getting the best of the argument.

Some children involved in theft incidents at Woolworth's were questioned in the school by the police today. The exhibitionist is still across the street and still no police have investigated him.

I saw Kenny and his mother on the street this afternoon after school. He has not been to school since Wednesday. He and his mother claim that he has no shoes, only a pair of sneakers.

I asked her to bring Kenny in Monday. She should be informed about her son's bad language, cheating, stealing from other children, and molesting little girls in the special classes.

• • •

MONDAY

April 29

The children were unusually noisy today.

Joe became ill and had to be sent home. His mother had given him pork chops, rice, and beans for breakfast, and all of it came up. His mother was not at home so we had to call the emergency number of a friend of hers and ask her to tell the mother to expect him home.

Neither Kenny nor his mother showed up today. I had not really expected them, but one always hopes.

• • •

TUESDAY

April 30

Kenny still has not come to school, nor has his mother visited or called me.

Joe is still out, probably because of his upset stomach.

Melvin's mother brought him to school to explain why he was absent a few days last week. She refers to him as "this boy."

"This boy didn't have no shoes, Mr. Haskins, so he didn't come."

When I asked her if she sent him to school, she replied, "Well, if this boy didn't want to come, I can't make him."

Another false fire alarm today.

• • •

WEDNESDAY

May 1

No music today. The music teacher had to go to the hospital for treatment of her bitten arm. It is still giving her a lot of trouble.

Several other teachers were out today. In one very difficult third-grade class the new substitute left at one-thirty. She walked out of the class, down the stairs, looking straight ahead, and out the door without saying why or signing out.

The pupils were standing on the desks and chairs, throwing crayons and books. The assistant principal had to take the class for the rest of the afternoon.

A girl in the fifth-year class came to school today after being out a few days. The reason she gave was that she had been to her aunt's funeral. It seems that the aunt dropped dead from drinking over the weekend, and was found by the superintendent of the building on Tuesday. The girl says that her aunt had a German shepherd dog who, as a result of not being fed, ate off one of her legs. The aunt's boyfriend killed the dog after this was found out.

• • •

THURSDAY

May 2

Melvin brought his younger brother to school today because his mother was going to have company (her friend, as he puts it).

The brother has been in Rockland State for the past year and his mother took him out without permission on Monday. Rockland was unable to reach the mother (no telephone) and called our guidance counselor because they knew he had a brother attending this school. The mother had tried to enroll the child at our school on Tuesday but was unsuccessful because there were no records and no release from Rockland.

I took the brother to the office, where he had to sit most of the day because we couldn't reach the mother and didn't have a family worker who could take him home.

Finally the police took the brother home.

• • •

FRIDAY

May 3

Kenny still has not been to school, nor has a 407 form, a phone call, or a letter from the principal's office produced his mother. We are hoping for Monday.

The playground is nearly ready—the cleanup is finished and all that is left now is the pouring of the concrete and the fence.

Now that it's spring, the broken windows are being replaced today.

A fifth-grade boy told the math teacher she had "an ugly, wrinkled white face." She repeated the remark to a black teacher, who asked her whether or not it was true. The math teacher said maybe it was, but the student should not be allowed to say it.

• • •

MONDAY

May 6

Sidney's mother came in to see me today, complaining that she can't do anything with him and is considering sending him to boarding school, which she cannot afford. She really means someplace like the Wiltwyck School for Boys, upstate.

A boy in another class was badly cut on the hand. No one in the room will say how it happened.

Kenny did not come to school today and Joe is out sick again with a stomach disorder.

Another false fire alarm today. The assistant principal waited until the fourth signal before he reported it false. By that time a good many classes were halfway down the stairs.

• • •

TUESDAY

May 7

I called Kenny's mother again about his continued absence. She pretended that I had the wrong number and no one by her name lived there. When I called the same number again, there was no answer.

Joe's mother brought him in and claimed the doctor said it must have been something he ate at school that threw his stomach out of whack. She asked me, "What kind of food do they feed the children here anyway?" overlooking the possibility that the pork chops, rice, and beans he had for breakfast might have done it.

I received a note from Melvin's mother. She does not remember his birth date. She has to file his summer-school form and asked me to fill it out for her.

Also a note from Helen's mother saying she had received the official letter concerning her daughter's behavior and had called the school but got a busy signal; if I still wanted to reach her, I should call her neighbor, whose telephone number she supplied.

I spoke to the guidance counselor about referrals for two children and about Kenny's continued absence. This counselor is new on the job and unfamiliar with the technical procedures.

• • •

WEDNESDAY

May 8

I took my class out of music today because of difficulties with the music teacher. She keeps reminding my children of the great favor she is doing them whenever they get the infrequent chance to have music.

I will give them music at the appointed time on Wednesdays and avoid a great deal of unnecessary criticism and abuse.

Neither Kenny nor his mother has come to school.

Melvin has not had his hair cut for months. I first thought he or his mother had decided to let it grow, since that is the current style. I wrote to her that his long hair was okay but that did not mean it had to be unkempt.

She replied:

> Mr. Askins,
>   I do not have any money to get *Melvin* a Hair *cut* untill I get my check.
>
> From
Mrs. Turner

• • •

THURSDAY
May 9

Wilbert broke a school window today. The children have only one short street to play in at lunchtime because 134th Street is closed for the playground construction. He felt very bad about the window, believing I was going to send a note to his mother. I assured him that I would not, and he calmed down.

The school was upset today about a sixth-grade girl's little brother, who was reported missing since yesterday. The sister went around to all the rooms asking the children if they had seen him. He had left home in the morning, never got to school, and didn't return home in the afternoon. The police couldn't find him.

It turned out that he was with his father, who does not live with the mother. The father at first denied that the boy was with him when the mother called. The mother remained very calm throughout the whole affair.

• • •

FRIDAY
May 10

The school decentralization proposals were the main topic of teacher discussion today. A kind of end-of-week buildup of fears and frustrations. The white teachers are generally against the project and the black teachers for it. There was a constant heated dialogue in the halls and during the lunch periods.

The white teachers still fear the loss of their jobs, or at least the possibility of reprisals and discrimination. The black teachers point out that this has long been their plight in the school system.

The whites point out that what is happening in Ocean Hill will happen all over the city if decentralization is adopted. They are writing to the Ford Foundation criticizing the Bundy report* and the foundation's role in the plan for community control. The black teachers are responding by writing letters supporting the foundation's efforts.

• • •

MONDAY
May 13

Lots of problems in school today, in addition to excessive teacher absenteeism. There were four false fire alarms during the day, two right after each other. The secretary announced them false, but too late to stop several classes from leaving their rooms.

No substitute would take one absent teacher's class.

A girl created a disturbance as I was going down the hall, and shouted several remarks my way, including "you black son of a bitch" and "motherfucker." I took her to the assistant principal,

*A report financed by the Ford Foundation to study community control. McGeorge Bundy is the head of the foundation.

and she kept telling him that her mother was not at home, so he might as well stop trying to call her. Everyone sort of gave up.

• • •

TUESDAY

May 14

We met with the CRMD supervisor today. He was not well informed about plans for our unit for next year. Many teachers' questions were unanswered, and after the meeting we were left with a feeling of complete hopelessness.

A girl in the sixth grade cursed the parent of a boy in the class. The teacher had sent for both parents after some difficulty between the two children, but only the boy's mother showed up. After school, the young lady followed the boy and his mother down the street, still cursing at them.

The parent is considering pressing charges against the girl. The principal has been informed and some action is pending.

I saw Joe's mother today. She explained that their electricity has been turned off for the past week, and that's why Joe hasn't been doing his homework.

• • •

WEDNESDAY

May 15

Today we went to the Museum of Natural History. Some of the parents did not dress their children presentably for the trip, even though they were informed several days ahead.

Hal tore his pants and they split from back to front. I tied his jacket around his waist to avoid an embarrassing situation.

Both Irene and Rachel had been out since last Friday, but this morning Irene came to school with her arm and thumb in bandages and a note from her mother that she had cut it badly and that since the cut hand is her writing hand, I shouldn't "expect any writing out of her."

Cherry's mother sent a message that the child had broken her glasses and she doesn't know when she can have them fixed.

A detective finally came to see me today about the exhibitionist I reported several months ago. He went over to the apartment to talk with the man. Since we cannot prove he is the one—we never saw his face—he cannot be arrested.

The Metropolitan Reading Test scores were returned today. The sixth grade did very well, scoring an average of two years above grade level. In general, the school is doing much better than in previous years.

• • •

THURSDAY

May 16

The miniskirted teacher in Junior Guidance has resigned to get married and a new teacher has come in. She seems to be an effective person, but she's taking over a difficult class at the end of the school year.

Another false fire alarm today. We haven't had a real fire drill in months.

Joe's mother sent a note—she has moved about two doors down from the old tenement.

• • •

FRIDAY

May 17

The children had a great time on a trip to the Brooklyn Botanical Gardens. But the bus driver drove off to attend to personal business and didn't come back until it was almost too late to return to school for the three o'clock dismissal. The worst of it was that our lunches were in the bus, and the hungry children became irritable.

We had to have a late lunch on the bus on our way back to the school. One lunch was missing. The bus driver said someone stole it while the bus was parked in downtown Brooklyn. However, we suspect the driver ate the lunch. The best one.

The bus affair was reported to the assistant principal, who we hope will report it to the bus company.

Kenny came to school too late to join the trip, and we had to leave Melvin because he was dressed so shabbily. He needs shoes badly. He says his mother is waiting until she gets her check to get him a new pair. Three welfare check days have gone by already.

• • •

MONDAY

May 20

Kenny came to school late this morning and went straight to the office for a late pass. When he was refused because they were "busy," he left the building.

Melvin was out today. His family's social worker called to discuss conditions at home and in school.

One of the math teachers was absent again today. She is on the verge of a breakdown. She's been out since Thursday on what she calls her "mental health days."

At last an official fire drill today!

I talked today with several teachers whose plans for next year do not include coming back to work here. A great many are trying to get transfers.

There's the normal number who will leave because they dislike staying in one place so long and need a change. There are those who are so dissatisfied with the bureaucracy, the conditions, classroom behavior, supplies, and personality problems with both children and staff that they will quit. But many seeking transfers will be unable to leave because of the Board's transfer policy and will be stuck in an unhappy situation, which is sure to affect the children.

• • •

TUESDAY
May 21

Melvin came to school today in his usual sad mess. He told me his mother would pick him up at noon to go shopping and to get his hair cut. He said she had kept him home yesterday to clean him up because the social worker was coming.

The social worker who called me about him said she had found him unusually clean and bright, but when the mother does not expect her the opposite is usually the case.

A teacher went out for lunch today and was hit in the face by flying glass when a firecracker in a bottle exploded in front of her on the street. She required three stitches under the eye.

• • •

WEDNESDAY
May 22

I received a note from Sidney's mother today:

Good morning
Mr. Haskins the reason Sidney was absent yesterday was because I was sick and there were no one to stay Home with me.

Sign
His mother
Mrs. Slade

Sidney has become very interested in little girls. His mother says she can't do a thing with him. A larger boy in the neighborhood beat him up when he discovered Sidney with his sister in the basement.

We had another false fire alarm today, but the boy was caught. He is retarded. But he is not the only culprit; for the most part, the fifth- and sixth-grade boys are responsible for the false alarms.

We stayed away from music today, doing the assignment in our own room.

• • •

THURSDAY

May 23

We haven't seen the exhibitionist since the detective called on him. The shade in his window is pulled all the way down now.

There was general chaos again today. The teacher of the very difficult fourth-grade class was absent again, and as usual, her class went around insulting the teachers who attempted to help out, since no substitute would take the class.

One male substitute told the assistant principal that he would go home rather than teach that class. Finally the class had to be broken up for the day.

• • •

FRIDAY

May 24

The playground is finished but so far no equipment has been installed. The children have started to use the area, but some still choose to play in the street. They have become accustomed to not having a playground.

A driver of the bus for the retarded children cursed at a little girl today. It was raining and she tried to open her umbrella as she was leaving the bus. The umbrella caught in the door and the driver was delayed for a minute or so. He has been reported to the principal.

• • •

MONDAY

May 27

Two false alarms today, one in the morning and one in the afternoon. Not only are those responsible seldom apprehended but the alarms seem to go off when the principal and the assistant principal are so far away from the p.a. system that by the time they reach it to announce a false alarm, half the classes are down the stairs.

A first-grade teacher called in this morning to say she was married yesterday and would be on her honeymoon until June 10. She did not inform anyone before this of her nuptial plans.

The carpenters finally arrived to fix the hall doors.

• • •

TUESDAY

May 28

Wilbert was hit by a car on his way to school this morning. We don't know how serious it is. It had been raining very hard since yesterday and some traffic lights had gone out. On the corner where he was struck, the traffic light was out and the cars and buses were taking their chances at the crossing.

Only half my students came to school today, probably because of the weather.

Another false fire alarm today. The principal took to the p.a. and complained that she was tired of this almost everyday occurrence, which she blamed on the laxity of the teachers who do not keep records of which students are out of the room. This infuriated many teachers, who feel that patrolling the halls is the responsibility of the parent aides.

• • •

WEDNESDAY

May 29

Nothing unusual today, just the general teacher absenteeism and the constant noise from the classes on the third floor.

The toilets on the second floor were broken today and the younger classes had to use the third-floor facilities. The overcrowding in the halls, as teachers brought their classes up for rest periods, created bedlam.

Tomorrow is Memorial Day. No work! Rest.

• • •

FRIDAY

May 31

One of the boys in the Junior Guidance class stole the teacher's check right out of her purse. He did not return to school after lunch. A parent aide went to his home and, with the boy's mother, searched the apartment. They found the check.

There was a notice at the time clock this morning:

My dear teachers:

I find that some absences are being taken without notifying us in advance. If you plan to be absent and have this knowledge in advance, it is imperative that we be notified of this. I would prefer that this should be done in writing.

The Principal

• • •

MONDAY
June 3

Wilbert is still out. His mother sent a note explaining that he has to stay home a few more days. Jesus is back after his customary three-day absence, with the usual note from his mother that he had a bad cold. He wore a pair of wet sneakers, with no socks. As usual, his hair was uncombed and his face unwashed.

Cherry told me that she and her mother slept in a car last night because her father was angry with her mother.

Teachers are leaving the school, some for personal reasons, others for new positions. About five more have decided but not yet announced that they too will be leaving.

Cherry lost her glasses again today.

• • •

TUESDAY
June 4

I received two notes from parents today:

Dear Mr. Askins
    Melvin was sick that I kept home he fell dawn and cut his hand.
                singe Marylee

Good morning
    Mr. Haskins the reason Sidney was absent June the 3rd was because I was sick, and there was no one to stay home with me.
                Sign
                Mrs. Slade

Wilbert is still out.

The toilets on the second floor are still broken. The odor from the backup is bad.

From the windows the children enjoyed a loud argument between two men on the street. The profanity was real gutter level.

A parent aide found Cherry's glasses in the playground area during lunch.

• • •

WEDNESDAY
June 5

Now that summer is here and the playground nearly finished, outdoor activities are our major problem.

On our way to the park on St. Nicholas Avenue and 135th Street today, we were approached by winos and other assorted characters on the streets.

They make for a very touchy situation. Should the teacher ask them to leave the children alone or try to ignore them? If the teacher is female, the "friendliness" is actually an attempt to pick her up. The children are amused by the whole thing.

On our way, we saw Wilbert in his window. He waved to us. He couldn't come down and we couldn't go up to him, there being too many of us.

We sent an Italian ice up to him from the corner store and proceeded to the park, each with an ice of his own.

When we returned from the park we made get-well cards for Wilbert. We will mail them tomorrow.

• • •

THURSDAY

June 6

Many students and teachers were out today because of the death of Senator Robert Kennedy. A good number of substitutes showed up, but not enough to cover all the classes, which were doubled or halved, loading up the subs with as many as forty-three students in this emergency.

One substitute, a young girl, was strictly Board of Ed. She was constantly counting to ten, to give the class the chance to "come to order." She had rough sixth-year class and did not have much luck with her counting.

Today's graffiti on the back wall of the school, in blue crayon—PAM THE LOVER OF 134TH ST. On the front wall, THIS SCHOL STINK. Under it, YA IN MORE WAY THAN ONE. In the gym, THIS SCHOOL IS FULL OF SHIT. HA, HA.

A fourth-year boy was accidentally knocked unconscious while playing during the lunch hour, but he wasn't seriously hurt.

A boy in the sixth-year class across from my room went home to get his brothers, both dropouts, to beat me up, because I restrained him from hitting the substitute teacher. The parent aides weren't able to stop them from coming up to the third floor, but they were stopped by a male teacher before they reached me.

Schools will be closed tomorrow.

• • •

MONDAY

June 10

Wilbert came back to school today and told the class all about his accident.

Several boys shot off firecrackers during the lineup in the gym after lunch.

The staff bulletin at the time clock this morning warned us

that "no student is allowed to carry heavy packages." It is against Board of Education policy, etc. It seems the principal caught a teacher having a kid carry a large bale of paper upstairs.

A little boy in one of the Junior Guidance classes tried again to commit suicide over the weekend. His teacher is awaiting a psychologist or psychiatrist for him.

One false fire alarm today, but the boy was caught.

• • •

TUESDAY
June 11

Kenny has been out the past four school days. His mother brought him in yesterday, but only to speak with the guidance counselor. He has been in the boys' youth house in the Bronx for stealing money from a candy machine with some other boys.

Another false alarm today—no one bothers anymore when the alarm rings.

The gym was very noisy at lunchtime and there were several fights. This is usual.

• • •

WEDNESDAY
June 12

Kenny is absent again today. He may be returned to the youth house for boys next week.

Sidney came to school today bruised on his arms and legs. He said his mother and father both whipped him because he broke a cigarette lighter. The parents had gone visiting, leaving him at home alone. He said they were "kind of drunk" when they returned.

• • •

THURSDAY

June 13

I received two notes from parents today:

> Mr. Haskins
> I am sorry that Kenny is late, and was absent Fri. But I am still trying to see my case worker. And it has to be before Wed. Thank you.
> Mrs. T. Smith

> Dear teacher
> Please excuse Rachel for being late I wole her up to late.
> Mrs. Harvey

Kenny is still waiting to go to court to find out whether or not he is to be returned to the boys' youth house.

A substitute teacher who came in at ten told the assistant principal she had to leave at two-thirty. She worked three hours and was paid forty-five dollars for the day!

Many teachers are angry about the freedom and autonomy the per diem substitutes enjoy. Some have threatened to quit and work as subs.

• • •

FRIDAY

June 14

The second floor is still using the restrooms on the third floor; the plumbers have not been able to unstop the line.

The school was in an uproar today, especially during the lunch hour; firecrackers were going off in the halls and in the gym.

This is always a rough time of year, particularly with the junior high students taking their finals, being let out half days, and returning to the elementary schools to visit their old teachers. This creates a lot of extra traffic and excitement.

• • •

MONDAY
June 17

The windows on the back side of the school which were still intact were broken over the weekend. There were rocks and broken glass on the floor when we came in.

The custodian has not bothered to put up guards on the windows, most of which were already broken and boarded up. If they are not fixed and guards placed on them, all the windows in the school will have to be boarded up by September.

Demonstrations at the school down the street are causing considerable absenteeism here. The parents won't let their children come to school because of all the police cars in the neighborhood.

• • •

TUESDAY
June 18

The principal will not request the music teacher to return next year because of her unsatisfactory behavior with the children and poor relationships with the teachers. She has been absent for the past few days, which creates difficulties in planning for the closing exercises at the school. In her absence the sixth-grade teachers have to rehearse the children without music. Reports have it that she was in a Seventh Avenue bar this morning and never got to school.

Joe has been out all week with a bad rash.

I watched drugs being sold in the house across the street today. Four rather young white men sat in a parked car, pretending it was out of order—they had the hood up. Finally their contacts arrived and they all went into the tenement and stayed for about fifteen minutes. They all left together, along with a white woman with a little girl.

• • •

WEDNESDAY
June 19

Melvin, who has been absent since Friday, came to school at lunchtime, to eat lunch, and then left.

I saw him in the street at three o'clock. He said his mother had not cooked breakfast and had told him to go to school for food. She kept him home to take care of his little brother (who is to be sent back to Rockland State) while she went out.

A man the principal has been having trouble with entered the school and dared her to call the police to have him put out. He insists upon teaching the drums to the boys here without permission to do so.

• • •

THURSDAY
June 20

There were a good number of fights in school today.

Many teachers are out on the Poor People's March to Washington. As usual, their substitutes were unable to control the children.

The sixth grade is rehearsing the graduation exercises without the music teacher. Her attendance is still erratic. The sixth-year teachers have found another teacher who plays the piano, and they are rehearsing with her. They plan to have her play at the exercises if the music teacher doesn't show up.

• • •

FRIDAY
June 21

Hal fell into a mud hole on our trip to Van Cortland Park today. We had to put him on the grass in the sun and scrape the mud off him before he could dry. He cried because he feared his mother would whip him. But the children had a great time.

A fourth-year boy spied a nickel on the 168th Street subway roadbed and jumped onto the tracks to get it, scaring all of us out of our wits.

Several children from other schools were lost or left stranded when they couldn't be found at departure time. We directed them back to the subway station, but we too had to leave and we don't know whether or not they found their classes or managed to get back to their schools

• • •

MONDAY
June 24

The UFT chapter met in the teachers' room to take up the music teacher's grievance against the principal for not rehiring her. The music teacher was present and named the teachers she said were responsible for her dismissal. It was pointed out that she herself brought on her troubles without any help from the teachers, although it is true that many teachers do not like her, mainly because of her attitude toward the children. She yells and calls them names.

Earlier today there was a flare-up between the music teacher and the sixth-grade teachers when she tried to get the sixth-grade students to boycott the exercises as a protest against her being fired. When the assistant principal tried to intervene, she blew up at him in front of the rehearsing children, who applauded and urged her on.

She was quite a sight, standing there shouting with tears in her eyes, to the accompaniment of the band playing the march from *Aida*.

I received a note from Joe's mother about his rash and his summer-camp plans.

• • •

TUESDAY

June 25

Melvin came to school with his hand all bandaged up and a form from Harlem Hospital stating that he has a fracture. He said his little brother sat on his hand.

The math teacher had difficulty with a fifth-grade boy and took him to the Guidance office at two-thirty. When school was out he followed the teacher all the way to the subway, calling her names and throwing rocks at her.

The Afro-Arts Cultural Center presented an outdoor concert for the students and parents in the school yard this afternoon. The large audience, including many people in the tenement windows across the street, was very responsive.

• • •

WEDNESDAY

June 26

The graduation exercises today were sad and beautiful. So many parents and relatives were on hand to witness the end of their youngsters' journey through elementary school that there was hardly any standing room.

The pride of parents who have gotten their children through a difficult year showed in the tears in their eyes.

They held in their arms younger brothers and sisters of the graduates. A little girl, catching sight of her sister in the line of march, shouted, "Look, Ma, there's Beulah!" Her sister waved back to her proudly.

• • •

THURSDAY
June 27

No classes today, but much activity—the teachers anxiously awaiting Friday, the children looking forward to vacation time, the sixth-year graduates presenting their autograph books for their favorite teachers to inscribe with the usual platitudes.

The teachers were busy cleaning up their rooms, taking down bulletin boards, and storing books. (We cannot get final paychecks until our rooms are certified in good order for the custodian to clean up over the summer.)

Teachers were busy exchanging addresses and phone numbers with colleagues they have not spoken to all year. Many will not be returning to this school, but they will find the same conditions elsewhere if they choose to remain in ghetto schools.

• • •

FRIDAY
June 28

The last day.

Today was scheduled for only half a day for the children. Most of the teachers went out for lunch and returned at one for their checks. Some left at once, but many lingered over the year's toil with those children who remained to say good-bye again.

Was it a good year? Have the children really derived any benefit from it? How much did they really learn? Certainly they didn't learn as much as they should have.

As I turned the corner at St. Nicholas Avenue and 134th Street a little boy came up to me.

"Mr. Haskins, what you going to do this summer?"

I told him that first I was going to rest, then I'd have to think about it. I hadn't made any plans.

I asked what he was going to do.

He was uncertain. "Camp, maybe. If not I'll just stay around all summer."

If he doesn't go to camp, it will be the usual summer in the teeming hot streets of Harlem; then the fall and school, with no summer worth remembering.

4
Nine Children

NINE CHILDREN

At the end of the school year I tried to record in biographical form the lifestyle of the children I had worked hardest with during the term, in order to give the reader a more complete picture of their individual needs, their family situations, and the lives these children are condemned to live.

Hal

Hal is a tall, handsome, well-dressed child of ten with a quick, peculiar quietness. He has immature visual motor coordination and has been on tranquilizers for as long as I have been his teacher. Some mornings his mother forgets to give him his pills, and on these days Hal is especially off and upsetting to the rest of the class in his role as a tough and prolific talker.

Hal's mother has been in and out of the hospital all year and is back in the hospital now. An affectionate child, Hal is handicapped by this situation.

The boy does not at first seem mentally retarded, but his sporadic speech gives him away. He will easily tell anyone about his nightly dreams, in many of which he is the hero and in which his female psychiatrist regularly appears.

Hal always has more money than the other children, many of whom bring nothing to school. His is a much more middle-class family, living in one of the city housing projects and not on welfare. His stepfather, a taxi driver, gives Hal money every morning or meets him on the corner at lunchtime. The family seems to be a very closely knit unit, even though on the school records Hal's mother's name differs from the father's. She never fails to respond to a note or call concerning her son.

In the year Hal has been with me he has shown greater improvement in self-discipline than with the previous teacher, a fact confirmed by his mother, the principal, and the teachers who have observed his behavior.

According to the psychologist's report when he came into my class, Hal was at the first-grade level in both reading and math. He knew the alphabet only to "L," counted by rote to twenty, and had no knowledge of addition, all probably the result of the previous teacher's rather permissive emphasis on arts and crafts and play. On the Stanford-Binet, Hal had a performance I.Q. of 79 and a full-scale I.Q. of 73, indicating a borderline level of functioning. (It has been my experience that many borderline cases function on a higher level than Hal had attained; this indicates a lack of positive attitude on the part of his previous teacher.)

The psychologist's report suggested that perhaps Hal was aphasic, meaning that he would have trouble with associations, etc. Shown a picture of a table leg, an aphasic child would respond, "chair," "arm," "stick."

I found no great amount of this with Hal, at least no more than among normal children when they are shown pictures of things they do not readily recognize.

Hal has been seeing a psychiatrist at Harlem Hospital and usually tells me about his sessions with her. He doesn't like her because "she is too fat and I don't like fat ladies." I tell him that his mother is fat, so does that mean he doesn't like his mother? He says, "Oh, that's different, she doesn't look fat to me." I ask, "How does she look?" He responds acutely, "Like my mother." He also doesn't like the psychiatrist because "she asks me a lot of funny questions."

Hal's reading level now is 2.5 (halfway between second and third grade), though his comprehension is less, and he can count to ten in Roman numerals and can subtract and divide. With all his problems, Hal is a highly motivated child, eager to learn and searching for approval and affection. He has not been retested as he should have been, and I am trying to get this done as soon as possible.

Cherry

Cherry is a friendly child who talks in a slow, halting voice. Immature for a child of ten, she had a psychological test four years ago and another one a year later, both indicating that she functions within the range of mentally retarded intellectual ability. She achieved a verbal I.Q. of 61 on the Wexler Intelligence Scale for Children (WISC).

On both testing dates Cherry was tested by the same psychologist, who used the same test and got the same scores each time.

Her mother has not seen Cherry since she turned her over to the city. Cherry's surname is that of an unconcerned foster parent whom the city pays a hundred dollars a month to care for her. The child is not properly cared for by this foster mother, who makes a living caring for other children as well. Cherry is responsible for bringing these smaller children to and from school. As a result, she herself has not been on time since she has been in my class.

Cherry needed glasses desperately, but her foster mother took her year after year to a local optometrist, who each time advised that the child did not need glasses, and charged ten dollars for the visit. Late this year Cherry did see a specialist, which was advised in the beginning, and got her glasses.

The child certainly does need them. Either that or she is suffering from some eye disease that causes her to see normally sometimes and abnormally most of the time. The psychologist offered no indication of any organic problems, but I have suggested to the Guidance office that an appointment be made with a neurosurgeon to determine what is really wrong, only to be told, "That is not the role of the teacher, the school, or the Guidance office."

Cherry is the slowest of all my fifteen pupils. The many chores she has to remember concerning the children she must escort to and from school is a contributing factor in her learning block. Significantly, she remembers the messages the different teachers give her for transmittal to her foster mother.

The foster mother has not come to see me about Cherry's problems, although she is constantly in the school with papers to be signed in order to get a new child or to have one discharged from her household or because one is ill. She is always too rushed for discussion. With her runaway voice and inability to stand still while she talks, I must walk with her, sometimes a block from school, if I am to get in any points.

Cherry says she told her foster mother I wanted her to help the child with homework assignments. The mother told her she doesn't have the time—"She says to go into the room and do it."

Even though Cherry had not yet mastered the first-level addition facts—the 1 plus 1 or 1 plus 2 kind of adding—I decided late in the year not to further frustrate Cherry by giving her homework. I am trying to enlist the aid of the resource teacher to help her individually in order to raise her level of adding. However, there has been a drastic improvement in her reading over the preprimer level—a rise to 1.5 to 2.0, depending upon which test score, the Metropolitan or the Reading Readiness, is more reliable—mostly through the use of sight words and picture cues. Apparently they have worked very well, possibly because she enjoys the word games we play in class.

Helen

Helen's referral problem was: "Learning difficulties and poor peer relations." She still has great difficulty in orienting herself to the class environment. She has yet to understand what is expected of her. She responds to instructions with a wide, staring expression. Some physiological imbalance is inferred from her moist hands and excessive perspiring. Her speech is characterized by a lisp and a husky voice pattern; she is undergoing speech therapy to correct this.

On the WISC, she earned a full-scale I.Q. of 56 and a verbal I.Q. of 55. Her performance I.Q. was 65, suggesting a generally uneven intellectual functioning. Her psychological report states: "Patterns on this test are suggestive of a possible underlying dysfunction of the central nervous system as the basis for retardation."

Unlike some others in the class, Helen is a true CRMD. There are, however, social, intellectual, and physical reasons for her retardation.

Her personality style moves from outright hostility to her peers to subtle unawareness in the classroom. She doesn't interact socially except when we have parties, at which she will go dancing and smiling off in a corner alone, although she will not refuse to dance with the other girls if she is asked. She almost never takes the initiative to ask one of them to dance.

Her walk suggests some physical deformity. At times she seems to have a kind of stoop.

She has poor work habits. In the previous class she would either walk out or start a fight out of the clear blue whenever she did not want to work. When I speak firmly to her, she will sometimes sulk and cry for fifteen or twenty minutes (her method of escape, to keep from having to deal with the problem of the moment). It sometimes works, depending upon my involvement with the rest of the class at the time. I usually come back to her later in an attempt to find out what is making her cry.

She requires more intensive individual attention and instruction.

Kenny

Kenny is a tall, lanky boy with a narrow face that makes him appear much older than his ten years. His referral problem was: "Kenny is not progressing in his school work." The summary of the psychologist's referral report indicated that he was "slow in his reactions, and he has difficulty in comprehending directions. Kenny is a dependent and vulnerable boy who needs help and protection." He had a full-scale I.Q. of 69, a verbal I.Q. of 72, and a performance of 71 on the WISC. Kenny could count only to ten and recognized a few letters and small words. He was recommended for a middle-track CRMD class.

Since 1965, Kenny as been in four different schools. He was transferred to my class after a brief stay in another CRMD class, in which he cursed the teacher, fought with pupils, tried extortion, and attempted to rape a small girl—all while the teacher stood by helplessly. Until his placement in that class, Kenny had been to school only forty days of the school year. His mother had given all the attendance teachers the usual excuses a parent offers when she believes her welfare checks will be cut off if the child is taken away: "He has been sick," "He had no shoes," "I was sick," "I sent him but I guess he has a mind all his own."

In his previous class Kenny considered it very important that he shouldn't miss a day, because he was the big boss in the room and his absence might cause him to lose the prestige he had worked hard to achieve by constantly roughing up the rest of the pupils. He would come to school even if he was sometimes as late as eleven o'clock, but in time for lunch. (The previous teacher kept making excuses for him, so no referrals to the guidance counselor were made.) From the reports of various teachers and guidance counselors it is apparent that Kenny is a boy in trouble.

Since Kenny has been with me I have talked with his mother twice. The first time, over the telephone, she sounded very much interested in Kenny's problems and gave the impression that she wanted to get at the causes of his behavior. The second time she came to school with Kenny's younger brother in her arms, and she smelled strongly of whisky. She spoke very freely of her feelings about Kenny. The first thing that came out very clearly—and it struck me as odd, since most mothers are reluctant to face the truth about their feelings for their children—was that Kenny was basically a "damn no-good child, just like his damn no-good father, who lies and steals all the time."

Rachel

Rachel, aged ten, is a tall child, well dressed, quiet, poised, and soft-spoken. This is contrary to the psychologist's referral report that she was short in stature, slow-thinking, and appeared restricted.

Rachel's referral problem was: "Appears unable to understand fully and follow directions; cannot learn." In 1966 she was in the third grade, yet on the wide-range achievement she scored a reading grade of 2.2 and an arithmetic grade of 2.7, placing her on par with or not far behind the city's average for ghetto children. That year her I.Q. was 68 with a mental age of 6.6. All this indicates that she was not so much mentally retarded as she was socially deprived.

Apparently overlooking these known factors, the psychologist reported, "Rachel reveals great difficulty in her attempts to copy a diamond, a developmental task expected of a seven-year-old child." Why should he expect her to perform as a seven-year-old when she tested only 6.6 mental age?

He further reported: "She has a tendency to hold her pencil somewhat awkwardly between her second two fingers." A habit, he fails to point out, that is common in retarded and normal children, as the observation of the writing habits of any class of thirty children in any school, wherever located, would indicate. The way a child holds a pencil generally depends upon who taught him and when he learned to use it.

Many ghetto children do not know what a pencil is until they come to school. They may never have seen their mother or father use one. Also, as in Rachel's case, many never go to kindergarten, particularly those children with a southern background, who come to school too old for kindergarten and are thrown right into the first grade without any introduction to such tools as the pencil or to what is expected of them in the first grade.

It is the white, middle-class teacher who calls upon the white, middle-class psychologist to make a "proper" evaluation of the deprived black child on the basis of a middle-class instrument of intelligence measurement, the Stanford-Binet test. This test proves what was expected of it in the first place—that the black child is retarded—and he is placed in a CRMD class with the stipulation that at the end of a year or two there will be another test to determine whether the child has been helped by this placement. From the start, this is a misdiagnosis, with the child being further retarded when he or she is placed, in most cases, with really retarded and brain-damaged youngsters.

This is not to say that Rachel is without problems. But had the psychologist attempted to put all the factors together, he would have determined that Rachel needed guidance and therapy, not placement in a slow class. With her 68 I.Q., Rachel is much brighter and in better control of herself than many others with 73 I.Q.'s. She is not a slow learner; rather, she learns at her own pace. Until she is able within herself to accept whatever facts we may be discussing, she does not retain them. When she can accept them, she grabs them and holds on. She is by far the brightest child in the class of fifteen and does quite well in her relationships with the other children.

She is a quiet child, but in her quietness she is observant and bright-eyed. In a special class that deprives her of the kind of relationships she should be experiencing with other boys and girls her own age, she is aware that she has to make the best of a bad situation, and she does. She associates with her peers outside the CRMD classroom and probably enjoys playing with them more than with some of the children in her own class.

In the final analysis, I expect that Rachel will return to a normal classroom situation, and I have submitted the request for her retesting.

Joe

Joe is a lively, energetic youngster with a pronounced speech defect. From the psychologist's report and my teaching experience with him, he is retarded. He has a full-scale I.Q. of 56 and a performance I.Q. of 65. After two years of speech therapy and CRMD placement, he is still deficient in his verbal expression, judgment, and concentration areas.

Joe has difficulty in recognizing the different aspects of situations. According to the psychologist's report, he was "able to identify some of the alphabet, but is not able to read any words. He does not recognize all the colors and can only count from one to eight." Joe now knows his alphabet, can count to a hundred, knows all the colors, and reads on about a 1.2 level.

The boy has never known his real father. He has lived with his mother in many different one-room flats in the same area, attending the same school. His mother does day work downtown; she is illiterate and in poor physical health, and recently had to have all her teeth pulled. She does her best to keep Joe neat and clean, and he does have a few extra cents to spend on himself.

He is proud on Fridays when he gets the chance to wear his white shirt to assembly. On these days he is all shiny and new looking and does not play with the other boys for fear they will get his shirt dirty. If they touch him he brushes himself and frowns.

Joe has a humped-over, old-man walk which he is unable to correct. He moves in long strides, swinging his arms wildly, when he is in a hurry. When I remind him that he has not combed his hair he tells his mother that he needs a haircut, even if he has had one the week before. He seems more eager to get his hair cut than to comb it. He has been going to a female barber, whose name he doesn't know, for a year or more.

His overall behavior within the class situation is good, even though he has great difficulty in expressing himself. This sometimes evokes laughter from the other children. When I ask him, "Joe, what did you like about the story I read, or didn't you like it?" he seems very confused, as if he is having trouble understanding plain English. His mother also has a speech defect but he seems able to understand her. To a phrase like "Say finger, Joe," he responds, "Inger"; to "Let Joe," his response is "Et."

When the class guest from Thailand gave the children postcards of the country's landmarks it was Joe who, after long thought, asked her for her zip code so he could write to her. When she explained that Thailand does not need zip codes because the country is very small, Joe said, "Ooks ig to me," (Looks big to me.)

The doctor who has checked Joe says the child's tongue is not

tied and there are no other physical defects. He is simply retarded and slow to learn. Possibly his early learning was based on
his mother's defective speech pattern and he finds it difficult to
change over, for fear he might be incapable of mastering the correct pronunciation and thereby lose all ability to communicate.

Joe is not sure of his present address. Like many children in
my class, he has his name and address on the cover of his composition book, which he will refer to when he is asked where
he lives.

Like all but three of my children, Joe has never had a telephone at home. During a class unit on the use of the telephone
he was excited at playing "emergency calls." He wanted to be the
policeman "because my father is." He was referring to his mother's
boyfriend, who is not a policeman but a security guard with a
police-like uniform. The police image evokes a fantasy world in
which Joe can project himself into some big, important position.

(Joe, like the other children, was reluctant to allow the others
to take their turns at the telephone. They enjoyed calling the fire
department and the police department but they had great difficulty understanding that they could not start talking until after
the phone at the other end of the room rang. I finally got them to
just dial "O" for operator and ask her to get whatever emergency
number they wanted to reach.)

Joe's mother came in during the winter to ask me for the
number to call to make her landlord give her some heat. I gave
her the emergency telephone number which was constantly in
the daily press and on radio and television.

It is clear that Joe's mother, through no basic fault of her own,
has been a major instrument contributing to his retardation, as is
the case of so many other parents of retarded children. Add the
factor of social deprivation resulting from his own lack of experience and we have some reason for a substantial portion of his
problems.

Little if anything can be done for his mother. She works long
and hard in order to support her son and herself. It looks hope-

ful that Joe can be helped to overcome many of his difficulties. He has made tremendous growth in important areas and is continuing to do so. He will need a lot of help. Some he will receive; some he will not, mainly because of the educational system's deficiencies.

Sidney

Sidney is a tall, dark, good-looking boy of eleven who was recommended for CRMD placement two years ago, after being placed on medical suspension and therapy at Harlem Hospital. In 1963 he had an I.Q. of 78 on the Binet. At that time, from the psychologists' evaluation, his greatest difficulty appeared to be motor coordination in writing and drawing. In a 1966 evaluation, Sidney achieved a verbal I.Q. of 72 and a performance of 76, arriving at a full scale of 74, which placed him in the borderline range of functioning. He had some problems which were more physical than emotional; the psychologist reported that he was "left-handed and right-eyed," and recommended that Sidney could benefit from a CRMD placement to give him "support and structure that are lacking in his life now."

Sidney's figure drawing and associations in the classroom seem to reflect his emotional problems. From the interview I had with his mother, it would appear that she is the cause of a great many of his frustrations. She believes that he does not achieve because he is lazy, and she treats him as such. At home, she regularly beats him when he does not do his homework.

I try not to give him homework that he will have difficulty with and that will get him a beating. I give him more difficult work at school, where failure to achieve the expectation level will not create trouble.

Sidney constantly daydreams when we have our reading or drawing lessons. Usually he almost immediately relates a word someone calls out or a picture someone is drawing to one of his experiences, and he is then lost in thought for the rest of the period. When questioned about it he is very eager to tell the class what he is thinking. In most cases what he is thinking is entirely unrelated to what we are reading or drawing. I try to let him talk it out, but usually this doesn't work because Sidney goes on and on once he gets started.

He is a very likeable child and gets on well with the others. He is the brightest (if that term is appropriate) of the boys, but not the most dependable. Even though he is aware of his responsibilities, he seems unwilling to accept them, probably because there is so much stress on him at home and he feels that school is the place to escape. His parents regularly leave him at home alone with his grandfather, who is the superintendent of the building they live in. He tells me he likes it when they leave, because then he can talk to "Gramps."

One incident has so affected him that he still has difficulty getting over it. He broke a cigarette lighter while his mother and father were out, and when they returned they beat him, "to teach him not to touch things that don't belong to him." Even though the lighter was a part of the household, he should not have touched it. Sidney has not been able to accept this occurrence. I've tried discussing it with him and he seems to understand it better now—his parents were both high, they had been drinking and were tired and were not completely responsible for their acts. Sidney is further disturbed because his father, who works nights, gives him complete inquisitions about men who might have visited his mother while he was away at work.

Lena

Lena is another one of the new children who came to me in September from another school. Her referral problem was: "Cannot follow routines."

Lena is an immature but friendly and cooperative child who appears confused by the classroom demands that are made upon her. She is eleven years old, and her mental age of 5.0, when she was tested four years ago, has probably been increased by two points. This is only an observational likelihood since she has not been retested since, even though the psychologist's report recommended she be retested after two years.

The psychologist found her I.Q. to be "66 with a limited range of achievement characterized by marked unevenness." The report suggested that she is a nonreader, which she probably was then. However, over the years she has achieved a 2.5 reading level—one more reason why follow-up reports on children in special classes should be intensified. In the system today there is usually no regular follow-up except by the teachers, who for the most part do not have records of recommended retest dates.

Lena's situation is not unique among CRMD children. Many who have been helped to progress from their borderline situations to function in normal classes do become "retarded" (if such a word is appropriate) if they remain in the CRMD class. Sometimes they are not retested even if the teacher is certain that the child is ready for a normal class. The teacher simply may not want them to move on to normal classes. (They may be the only children in the class who can learn and thus can stimulate the teacher to really teach; such teachers will not refer them because "If they leave me, I'll have no one to teach.")

This may have been the case with Lena, who has shown remarkable progress and self-control since she has been with me. She is able to concentrate and do as much abstract thinking as many "normal" children.

Like so many other children here, Lena has many social problems, in addition to those of her own personality. She lives with a foster mother; her own mother died when she was a baby. (I don't think Lena is aware of this.)

She is a physically weak little girl who apparently never gets enough to eat. Her excuse, when she admits that she has had no breakfast, is usually a lie, but I never press her because she has been told long ago to tell her teachers, "I had to catch the bus so I didn't have time." The real reason is that the parent did not get up in time to cook breakfast, or that if there were breakfast there would be no food for dinner. The children at least get lunch at school.

As with most ghetto children, Lena has learned to lie and really believe her lies. She's been telling lies so long, she has learned to lie to get along. This is a lesson all ghetto children learn at a very early age.

I have not met her foster mother, although I have sent her numerous notes and mailed letters asking her to come in and at least discuss Lena's hygiene problems. Apparently the mother never sees the child when she leaves for school in the morning; if she did, she would certainly give Lena some tissues so she could blow her nose.

Lena has a constant cold. She hasn't been without one all year. The mother must be aware of this. Lena's lips are constantly chapped and she has a low-running fever, which the school nurse said is not dangerous but should be checked. If only we could get the mother to take the child to a clinic! Lena explains the cold as a result of not having much heat in the house at night.

Lena comes to school smelling as if she has wet her bed. She tells me she doesn't, but that she sleeps with her little sister who does. She can't help her body odor because she sometimes sleeps in her clothes when there is no heat. When the odor became unbearable for the rest of the children, the resource teacher took her in hand and showed her how to wash up. A deodorant was bought for her, as well as some Vaseline, which I gave her for her chapped lips and the rough spots around her mouth and nose. I asked the resource teacher to write to the mother and suggest that she see to it that Lena bathes every night. There was no answer.

I was able to get Lena's glasses fixed. Since October she had been coming to school with one temple piece of her glasses taped up to keep it from falling off. Her mother kept taping it at home and I was taping it in school amid a continuous flow of notes home and pink slips to the nurse to get Lena new frames. In March, Lena came in with the glasses fixed, after she had been coming to school a week without them. Ironically, she had a new brown temple which did not match the white frame. The right temple finally went too, and we started all over on the long process of getting new frames. We finally succeeded.

I can't allow myself to believe the new frames were even a marginal victory for me, because the lack of glasses may have been more of an irritant to the mother than to me. Lena is virtually blind without her glasses and was probably bumping into the other children at home.

I have found that parents usually do things for these children only when what they do increases their own use of the child. Lena tells me that she hates going home because from the moment she arrives all she does is wait hand and foot on her mother, who sits in front of the television set. Lena herself almost never sees a complete television program because her mother has her constantly on the run, bringing her beer and fruit and putting up the dinner. Lena finds humor in mocking her mother, but apparently there is also great hostility in her.

Lena is a crier. She has a rebellious nature and an almost total disregard for her peers. She will start fights among them and then pretend not to know how they started. When she is caught in the middle or the fight turns on her, she'll run to me or the nearest teacher for help.

Lena reads well, but has trouble with story endings. In some cases she'll make substitutions for words—for "house" (which she does know; I have had her learn to spell and pronounce it) she sometimes says "building." She knows the meaning of both "building" and "house" and pronounces each word correctly.

Lena probably will be retested later this year or next year, depending upon when the district supervisor acts on the referral information and when the Bureau of Child Guidance gets around to it. I expect that she will be placed in a normal class and be able to function with children her own age. But at present Lena is not ready socially, because of her inability to interact on what is considered the normal level. Tremendous progress in this area will have to be made, and her next teacher can expect no help from Lena's foster mother.

Wilbert

Wilbert is a cute, lively youngster who, before he came to me, had temper tantrums to get his way. He is eleven years old. The psychologist says that Wilbert has an I.Q. of 69 and a test age of 5.6, which indicates borderline intellectual ability. The psychologist suggests that Wilbert is an "immature, overly sensitive youngster who is apparently keenly aware of his inability to achieve more successfully both in school and at home," and this, of course, interferes with his intellectual functions.

Had the psychologist been more aware of the boy's home life, possibly he would not have been so eager to place him in a CRMD class; even in his own report, Wilbert is a borderline case.

Wilbert is the oldest of four children, the baby six months old, a sister in the third grade, and a younger brother in Junior Guidance because of his inability to sit still. This brother picks on Wilbert constantly and beats him up whenever he has a mind to. Although he is older, Wilbert is smaller and weaker than his sister and brother.

Wilbert's father has had five serious operations and has not been able to work in many years. He is in bed most of the time, and the family burden is on the mother. The father's anger and frustration because of his inability to work and be master of his home apparently are taken out on the children when he feels strong enough to assert himself. On many occasions Wilbert has come to class frightened and hungry because his father made him leave the house without breakfast for any number of petty reasons.

I spoke to the father once when he was feeling well enough to come to school and another time when I visited after school to observe the home situation myself. On these occasions he told me that he is very ill most of the time but when he feels better he whips the children "to make up for both old and new badness." I tried to explain that this only creates deeper fears of him in the children. He shrugged his shoulders, as if to say, "What can I do? I do my best." The answer to this man's problems is not an easy one, but the basis of the relationship between him and his children will have to come from him. They are in desperate need of guidance that they are not getting from the school, although the mother is open to suggestions and is constantly in school meetings with the counselors.

She wrote the following letter to Wilbert's previous teacher:

Dear Mrs.————

Did not know that Wilbert had started crying again. Am very sorry and disatisfied with Wilbert about his self control. I really got down on him about it Because I know he knows better. Please let me know if he does not improve. Because this is something I really don't like at all.

Sincerely,
Williams

At first Wilbert would remove his shirt and shoes in a huff and dash out of the classroom and into the halls, yelling and screaming as if someone were after him. He would end up in the principal's office, crying until his face would swell. All the clerks in the office knew Wilbert and kept a supply of candy on hand for when he would act up.

For a time Wilbert continued to receive this kind of preferential treatment. He even ate his lunch in the general office. This was in the days when permissiveness was the watchword. Everyone was afraid that something terrible would happen if Wilbert was denied his special privileges. It took a lot of disapproving to get the office clerks to stop catering to his whims. When Wilbert realized that he would no longer receive special treatment, he slowed down on his trips to the office, but not his flights out of the classroom.

He finally realized, too, that the other teachers had their own problems and would close their doors to shut out his noise. This was achieved in accordance with a plan I had worked out with the teachers. He would then find his way slowly back to the classroom and stand in the doorway. When I did not welcome him with open arms and halt class activities to ask him in, he would quickly move to his seat and stay there, not doing any work but staring and trying to figure me out.

Eventually Wilbert came to understand that there were others in the class who also needed my help. He finally acclimated himself to class participation and is doing well now. He has gained self-control and his reading and math have improved. Now Wilbert has been retested and, I hope, will be assigned to a regular class.

He is well motivated and seemingly delights in his newfound confidence in himself. This attitude has offset many of the problems he has at home. Recently, when a fire in his building kept all the children out of school, Wilbert cried, his mother reported, until she had to agree to send him to school at noon.

Wilbert probably benefited from the small-class situation, but not much from the CRMD class itself. He could have been severely retarded if steps had not been taken to stop his tantrums and get him engaged in meaningful work. Wilbert was not so much retarded as he was socially deprived, rather like Rachel. All the human material was there to work with but because of his limited knowledge about himself and things and the people around him, he was at first unable to make the kinds of associations so necessary to survive in a school of a thousand and classes of some thirty-five children each.

He is luckier than many other very disturbed children, who go thorugh elementary school undetected, sometimes because they are never reported by the teacher, sometimes because there are too many forms to fill out, or because of fear of confrontations with parents who, learning that the teacher has referred their son or daughter for psychological testing, sometimes protest violently.

Afterword

I went back to PS 92 a few years ago. If anything, the neighborhood seemed more blighted than before. The men who could
not find work still sat and stood around the stoops, and there was
no reason at all to move, since there was no new construction in
the area. The playground, whose construction the stoop men had
aided in their way while I was teaching at PS 92, looked twice as
old as it actually was. The wire fence, new when I taught there,
was broken and full of holes, the concrete potholed and strewn
with glass. The school itself was covered with graffiti, and it was
hard to realize that the graffiti explosion is a relatively new phe-
nomenon. Certainly there was some ten years back, but one
never saw entire walls covered with this "urban art" back then.

The complexion of the student population had changed very
little; non-blacks were still a small minority. Nor had the racial
mix of the teaching staff changed very much, although some of
the teachers themselves had changed. The teachers I remembered as young and erect and full of energy and dreams were,
like the older teachers who were there when I was on the staff,
tired and uninterested and seemed to look forward only to retire-
ment (In 1978, the city's fiscal crisis having eased, the Board of
Education announced that it could rehire a large number of
these teachers who had been laid off three years earlier. But
most of the former teachers did not wish to return. Once they
had accepted the fact of being laid off, they discovered that they
were relieved to be free of the endless frustrations of too-large
classes of ill-prepared children and not enough supplies and
mountains of bureaucratic paperwork and destructive racial and

political tensions. The children are not the only victims of the urban school system.)

The children I saw at PS 92 that day were all strangers, of course, but I have seen two of my former students in the past few years. I met one on the sidewalk in front of a supermarket about ten blocks north of the school. He was unloading cartons from a delivery truck, part of his job as a stock clerk at the store. Although he was of high school age, he had quit school at the age of sixteen rather than go on to a vocational high school or to a special class in a general studies high school. He knew of only two of his former classmates who had not quit school upon reaching legal age. Manifestly, none would attend college, although I believe that the second former student I encountered was bright enough to do so.

While walking along West 145 Street one night, I became aware that someone was coming up quickly behind me. I turned to confront two teenagers in sneakers who, I am certain, planned to rob me. One was my former student. Recognition flashed across his face, and he fled with his cohort. So, one of my kids became a mugger. He was an intelligent youth, an example of my contention that a lot of urban ghetto children who are labeled retarded are merely culturally and socially deprived. Under different circumstances, this boy might have had a promising future, and the greatest tragedy of the urban ghetto school system is this waste of talent and energy.

I had hoped, going to PS 92, that I would see some evidence of progress, some encouraging sign that things were better. But why should one school deviate from the general state of urban education in this country, and why should we expect the education of blacks to be any better when the housing of blacks, the employment of blacks, and the social status of blacks remains essentially unchanged? The Kerner Commission finding that there are two Americas, one black and one white, still obtains. It appears that, rather than making progress, we have slid backward; indeed, white America seems eager to return to the way it was before 1960, to the good old days before it has a conscience. One need only consider the Bakke decision, the Weber case in Louisiana, the Sears, Roebuck suit concerning affirmative action, and the recent Department of Labor statistics on unemployment among blacks to see that the nostalgia craze has not been confined to *Grease* and large weddings and pegged pants.

It has certainly invaded the educational sphere. The prevailing wisdom nowadays seems to be that all the brave new experiments were tried and did not work. I say that white America lost its sense of commitment, which was not wholehearted at the outset. The truly revolutionary proposals, like the voucher system and teacher accountability, were never even tried.

More blacks are attending college today than ever before, but they still feel alienated on majority-white campuses. Most black children still attend segregated elementary, middle, and high schools, and northern cities like Boston and Philadelphia have erupted into racial battlegrounds over the issue of school desegragation while the so-called defiant South has looked on in disbelief. We have seen the erosion of black staff and faculty and the closing down of black studies departments at colleges and universities, while departments devoted to other ethnic studies are established and flourish with the kind of funding that ensures success. We have seen state and local courts, faced with charges that whites are being discriminated against in favor of blacks, respond to those charges far more quickly than they ever did when blacks were being discriminated against; where is the concept of "all deliberate speed" now?

In short, we were wrong to believe that the clock cannot be turned back. It's a naive image anyway. Human beings make clocks and human beings create the conditions under which they will live—and the majority rules. The majority of us turn clocks back every fall, at the end of Daylight Savings Time, and it appears that the time in the sun for blacks in this country is coming to an end just as inevitably.

ALSO AVAILABLE FROM THE NEW PRESS

Being with Children:
A High-Spirited Personal Account of Teaching Writing, Theater, and
Videotape
Phillip Lopate

A new edition of Lopate's classic account of his relationship to his writing craft and to his young students, with a foreword by Herbert Kohl.

978-1-59558-337-6 (pb)

Beyond the Bake Sale:
The Essential Guide to Family-School Partnerships
Anne T. Henderson, Karen L. Mapp, Vivian R. Johnson, Don Davies

A practical, hands-on primer on helping schools and families work better together to improve children's education.

978-1-56584-888-7 (pb)

Black Teachers on Teaching
Michele Foster

An oral history of black teachers that gives "valuable insight into a profession that for African Americans was second only to preaching" (*Booklist*).

978-1-56584-453-7 (pb)

The Case for Make Believe:
Saving Play in a Commercialized World
Susan Linn

From the author of *Consuming Kids*, a clarion call for preserving play in our material world—a book every parent will want to read.

978-1-56584-970-9 (hc)

City Kids, City Schools:
More Reports from the Front Row
Edited by William Ayers, Gloria Ladson-Billings, Gregory Michie, and Pedro Noguera

This new and timely collection has been compiled by four of the country's most prominent urban educators to provide some of the best writing on life in city schools and neighborhoods.

978-1-59558-338-3 (pb)

City Kids, City Teachers:
Reports from the Front Row
Edited by William Ayers and Patricia Ford

A classic collection exploding the stereotypes of city schools, reissued as a companion to *City Kids, City Schools.*

978-1-56584-051-5 (pb)

The Color of Wealth:
The Story Behind the U.S. Racial Wealth Divide
Meizhu Lui, Bárbara Robles, Betsy Leondar-Wright, Rose Brewer, and Rebecca Adamson

An eye-opening field guide to the wealth gap by five leading experts.

978-1-59558-004-7 (pb)

Coming of Age in America:
A Multicultural Anthology
Edited by Mary Frosch with a foreword by Gary Soto

The acne and ecstasy of adolescence, a multicultural collection of short stories and fiction excerpts that *Library Journal* calls "wonderfully diverse from the standard fare," in a beautiful new edition.

978-1-56584-147-5 (pb)

Coming of Age Around the World:
A Multicultural Anthology
Edited by Faith Adiele and Mary Frosch

Twenty-four stories by renowned international authors chronicle the modern struggle for identity among young people around the globe.

978-1-59558-080-1 (pb)

Consuming Kids:
The Hostile Takeover of Childhood
Susan Linn

In this shocking exposé, Susan Linn takes a comprehensive and unsparing look at the demographic advertisers call "the kid market," taking readers on a compelling and disconcerting journey through modern childhood as envisioned by commercial interests.

978-1-56584-783-5 (hc)

Crossing the Tracks:
How "Untracking" Can Save America's Schools
Anne Wheelock

A groundbreaking survey of schools around the country that have success-fully "crossed the tracks" and reintegrated their classrooms.

978-1-56584-038-6 (pb)

Dismantling Desegregation:
The Quiet Reversal of Brown v. Board of Education
Gary Orfield and Susan E. Eaton

"Powerful case studies . . . the authors convincingly argue that the ideal of desegregation is disappearing." —*Kirkus Reviews*

978-1-56584-401-8 (pb)

Everyday Antiracism:
Getting Real About Race in School
Edited by Mica Pollock

Leading experts offer concrete and realistic strategies for dealing with race in schools in a groundbreaking book that should become required reading for every teacher in the country.

978-1-59558-054-2 (pb)

Final Test:
The Battle for Adequacy in America's Schools
Peter Schrag

An in-depth look at "the brave new world of school finance" (*Education Week*) and the latest struggle for equality in public education, *Final Test* describes a powerful new movement that has emerged across America in recent years to bridge the wide gap still separating the achievement of African American and Latino students from their white and Asian counter-parts more than half a century after *Brown v. Board*.

978-1-59558-026-9 (pb)

Fires in the Bathroom:
Advice to Teachers from High School Students
Kathleen Cushman

This groundbreaking book offers original insights into teaching teenagers in today's hard-pressed urban high schools from the point of view of the students themselves. It speaks to both new and established teachers, giving them first-hand information about who their students are and what they need to succeed.

978-1-56584-996-9 (pb)

Fires in the Middle School Bathroom:
Advice to Teachers from Middle Schoolers
Kathleen Cushman and Laura Rogers

Following on the heels of the bestselling *Fires in the Bathroom*, which brought the insights of high school students to teachers and parents, Kathleen Cushman now turns her attention to the crucial and challenging middle grades, joining forces with adolescent psychologist Laura Rogers.

978-1-59558-111-2 (hc)

Going Public:
Schooling for a Diverse Democracy
Judity Renyi

An informed overview of the multicultural education debate—of the formation and reformation of the canon, the call for a return to basics, and the politics of inclusion.

978-1-56584-083-6 (hc)

How Kindergarten Came to America:
Friedrich Froebel's Radical Vision of Early Childhood Education
Bertha von Marenholtz-Bülow

An enchanting 1894 account of the inventor of kindergartens, introduced to a new generation of educators and parents by Herbert Kohl.

978-1-59558-154-9 (pb)

Inequality Matters:
The Growing Economic Divide in America and Its Poisonous Consequences
Edited by James Lardner and David A. Smith

Leading American scholars and activists explore the question our leaders have been working overtime to ignore.

978-1-59558-175-4 (pb)

Islam Explained
Tahar Ben Jelloun

In an accessible question-and-answer format, *Islam Explained* clarifies the main tenets of Islam, the major landmarks in Islamic history, and the current politics of Islamic fundamentalism.

978-1-56584-897-9 (pb)

"I Won't Learn from You":
And Other Thoughts on Creative Maladjustment
Herbert Kohl

The now-classic piece on refusing to learn as well as other landmark Kohl essays.

978-1-56584-096-6 (pb)

Made in America:
Immigrant Students in Our Public Schools
Laurie Olsen

With a new preface by the author, this timely reissue probes the challenges facing teachers and immigrant students in our public schools.

978-1-59558-349-9 (pb)

May It Please the Court:
Courts, Kids, and the Constitution
Edited by Peter Irons

Sixteen Supreme Court cases on the constitutional rights of teachers and students involving school prayer, library censorship, political protest, and corporal punishment.

978-1-56584-613-5 (boxed set: HC with 4 cassettes)

The New Education:
Progressive Education One Hundred Years Ago Today
Scott Nearing

Classic vignettes, interviews, and speculations on school restructuring, curriculum development, and educational reform by a high-profile public advocate, with a foreword by Herbert Kohl.

978-1-59558-209-6 (pb)

The New Press Education Reader:
Leading Educators Speak Out
Edited by Ellen Gordon Reeves

The New Press Education Reader brings together the work of progressive writers and educators—among them Lisa Delpit, Herbert Kohl, William Ayers, and Maxine Greene—to discuss the most pressing and challenging issues now facing us, including schools and social justice, equity issues, tracking and testing, combating racism and homophobia, and more.

978-1-59558-110-5 (pb)

Other People's Children:
Cultural Conflict in the Classroom
Lisa Delpit

In this anniversary edition of a classic, MacArthur Award–winning author Lisa Delpit develops ideas about ways teachers can be better "cultural transmitters" in the classroom, where prejudice, stereotypes, and cultural assumptions breed ineffective education.

978-1-59558-074-0 (pb)

The Public School and the Private Vision:
A Search for America in Education and Literature
Maxine Greene

A newly updated edition of the celebrated educational philosopher's first masterpiece, with a foreword by Herbert Kohl.

978-1-59558-153-2 (pb)

Race:
How Blacks and Whites Think and Feel About the American Obsession
Studs Terkel

Based on interviews with over one hundred Americans, this book is a rare and revealing look at how people feel about race in the United States.

978-1-56584-989-1 (pb)

Racism Explained to My Daughter
Tahar Ben Jelloun

The prizewinning book of advice about racism from a bestselling author to his daughter, introduced by Bill Cosby. The paperback version includes responses from William Ayers, Lisa Delpit, and Patricia Williams.

978-1-59558-029-0 (pb)

Rethinking Schools:
An Agenda for Change
Edited by David Levine, Robert Lowe, Robert Peterson, and Rita Tenorio

The country's leading education reformers propose ways to change our schools, "cutting through the jargon and addressing the real issues" (Jonathan Kozol).

978-1-56584-215-1 (pb)

A Schoolmaster of the Great City:
A Progressive Educator's Pioneering Vision for Urban Schools
Angelo Patri

Angelo Patri's eloquent 1917 chronicle of multicultural education in the inner city remains as relevant today as it was ninety years ago, with a foreword by Herbert Kohl.

978-1-59558-212-6 (pb)

She Would Not Be Moved:
How We Tell the Story of Rosa Parks and the Montgomery Bus Boycott
Herbert Kohl

From a prizewinning educator, a meditation that reveals the misleading way generations of children have been taught the story of Rosa Parks, offering guidance on how to present the Civil Rights movement to young students.

978-1-59558-127-3 (pb)

Should We Burn Babar?:
Essays on Children's Literature and the Power of Stories
Herbert Kohl

The prizewinning educator's thoughts on the politics of children's literature.

978-1-59558-130-3 (pb)

The Skin That We Speak:
Thoughts on Language and Culture in the Classroom
Edited by Lisa Delpit and Joanne Kilgour Dowdy

A collection that gets to the heart of the relationship between language and power in the classroom.

978-1-59558-350-5 (pb)

Stupidity and Tears:
Teaching and Learning in Troubled Times
Herbert Kohl

"Vintage Kohl—incisive, funny, reflective, profound . . . a provocation to educators to better teach all our children."—Norman Fruchter, NYU Institute of Education and Social Policy

978-1-56584-982-2 (pb)

Teachers Have It Easy:
The Big Sacrifices and Small Salaries of America's Teachers
Daniel Moulthrop, Nínive Clements Calegari, and Dave Eggers

The bestselling call to action for improving the working lives of public school teachers—and improving our classrooms along the way.

978-1-59558-128-0 (pb)

Teaching for Social Justice:
A Democracy and Education Reader
Edited by William Ayers, Jean Ann Hunt, and Therese Quinn

A popular handbook on teaching for social justice for parents and educators.

978-1-56584-420-9 (pb)

"A Totally Alien Life-Form":
Teenagers
Sydney Lewis

More than fifty teens are interviewed and talk candidly about sex in the age of AIDS, violence at home and on the street, politics, race relations, education, and religion.

978-1-56584-283-0 (pb)

The View from the Oak:
The Private Worlds of Other Creatures
Herbert Kohl with Judith Kohl

The National Book Award–winning book on ethology: the study of the way animals perceive their environment.

978-1-56584-636-4 (pb)

Zero Tolerance:
Resisting the Drive for Punishment in Our Schools
Edited by William Ayers, Bernardine Dohrn, and Rick Ayers

A clear-eyed collection that takes aim at the replacement of teaching with punishment in America's schools.

978-1-56584-666-1 (pb)